THE SIX LAMPS

According to modern lineage holders of this tradition, reading and studying such material is perfectly fine, but applying it in practice requires formal transmission and authorization from a qualified master.

THE SIX LAMPS

Secret Dzogchen Instructions
of the Bön Tradition

Jean-Luc Achard

Wisdom

Wisdom Publications
199 Elm Street
Somerville, MA 02144 USA
wisdomexperience.org

Library of Congress Cataloging-in-Publication Data
Names: Achard, Jean-Luc, author. | Tapihritsa, 8th century. Sgron ma drug gi gdams
    pa. English.
Title: The six lamps: secret Dzogchen instructions of the Bön tradition / Jean-Luc
    Achard.
Description: Somerville, MA: Wisdom Publications, 2016. | Includes bibliographical
    references and index. | Includes translations from Tibetan.
Identifiers: LCCN 2016029291 (print) | LCCN 2016055280 (ebook) | ISBN
    9781614293644 (pbk.: alk. paper) | ISBN 1614293643 (pbk.) | ISBN
    9781614293804 (ebook) | ISBN 9781614293804 () | ISBN 1614293805 ()
Subjects: LCSH: Tapihritsa, 8th century. Sgron ma drug gi gdams pa. | Rdzogs-chen.
    | Bon (Tibetan religion)—Doctrines.
Classification: LCC BQ7980.2 .A25 2016 (print) | LCC BQ7980.2 (ebook) | DDC
    294.3/420423—dc23
LC record available at https://lccn.loc.gov/2016029291

ISBN 978-1-61429-364-4   ebook ISBN 978-1-61429-380-4

25 24 23 22
5 4 3 2

The cover image of Shitro is courtesy of Himalayan Art, himalayanart.org. Cover
design by Gopa & Ted 2, Inc. Interior design by Jordan Wannemacher. Set in Dia-
critical Garamond Pro 10.65/15.5.

Printed in the United States of America.

MIX
Paper from
responsible sources
FSC® C005010

Please visit fscus.org.

Contents

PART ONE. INSTRUCTIONS ON THE SIX LAMPS
Extracted from the Oral Transmission of the Great
Perfection in Zhangzhung

PART TWO. COMPLEMENTARY INSTRUCTIONS

Acknowledgments

The *Instructions on the Six Lamps* (*sGron ma drug gi gdams pa*) is one of the main root-texts of the *Zhang-zhung Nyengyü* series of teachings. It is considered the central work of the inner cycle (*nang skor*) of these teachings, mostly dealing with the principles of the natural state and its visionary marvels. In this respect, and even though the expressions themselves are not used in the original work, the root-text describes the teachings of Trekchö (*khregs chod*) and Thögel (*thod rgal*) as they were revealed by Tapihritsa to Gyerpung Nangzher Löpo.

In the course of preparing the translation and the material making up the present volume, I have been blessed with the generous help of several individuals without whom the book would never have seen the light of day.

Foremost among them are Marianne Ginalski and Michael Hunt, who have repeatedly and generously offered their precious time to read and check this volume in its various stages, providing on numerous occasions inspiring improvements, as well as corrections and suggestions that have greatly contributed to the legibility of the various parts of this book. Their contribution to the present volume is thus invaluable.

I would also like to send my heartfelt thanks to Henk Blezer, Gerd Manusch, and Kurt Keutzer, who kindly and spontaneously shared with me some scans of rare editions and manuscripts of the *Zhangzhung Nyengyü* that I would have been unable to access without their generosity. Their works on the history of the Bönpo tradition as a whole—both in academic and nonacademic circles—and on the *Zhangzhung Nyengyü* in particular have also been very inspiring.

My deepest gratitude goes here to the fantastic crew of the Wisdom Publications staff for their invaluable editing work, among them Laura Cunningham, Lydia Anderson, Ben Gleason, Andy Francis, and Daniel Aitken. Thanks also to the indexer, L. S. Summer.

It also goes without saying that Yongdzin Rinpoche has played a decisive role in the diffusion of this text, as well as in its correct, authentic understanding. I would thus like to dedicate the publication of this volume to Rinpoche's long life and to the continuation of his teaching activities.

                                                      Jean-Luc Achard
                                                Serling Dechen Ritrö

Introduction

The *Instructions on the Six Lamps* (*sGron ma drug gi gdams pa*) is one of the four major works belonging to the collection known as the Oral Transmission of the Great Perfection in Zhangzhung (*rDzogs pa chen po zhang zhung snyan rgyud*), the main Dzogchen cycle studied and practiced in the Bönpo school:[1]

- The first work is the *Twelve Son-Tantras* (*rGyud bu chung bcu gnyis*) from the first division of the *Zhangzhung Nyengyü*.[2]
- The second corresponds to the present text of the

---

1. On the contents and structure of the various editions of this collection, see Achard, *La Structure du Zhangzhung Nyengyü*. See also Kurt Keutzer, *Texts of the Zhang zhung snyan rgyud Cycle of Teaching*; Achard, *The Basic Structure of the Zhangzhung Nyengyü According to the Menri Edition*.

2. See its critical edition and translation in D. Rossi, *The Philosophical View of the Great Perfection of the Bonpos*, pp. 79–161.

Six Lamps, the main work of the second division of the cycle.[3]

- The third is the *Precepts in Eight Chapters*,[4] the one and only text of the third division of the cycle.[5]
- The fourth is the *Twenty-One Seals*, the central text of the fourth division of the cycle.[6]

As one will see below, the main themes of the *Instructions on the Six Lamps* are centered around the teachings dealing with the

---

3. There already exist several translations of this text into Western languages, the first one being the French translation I published in 1991 at Khyung-mkhar (together with the three other root-texts of the collection; see the references in the bibliography under *Les Quatre Cycles de la Transmission Orale*, pp. 35–59). The root-text of the *Six Lamps* was then reprinted alone in *Les Instructions sur les Six Lampes* (Khyung-mkhar, 1996). Since then, other versions have appeared. I am aware of Kurt Keutzer's English translation (including the Tibetan text and the commentary by Dru Gyelwa). Inger Olson has also prepared a translation of the root-text of the *Six Lamps* for her PhD (still unpublished and which I have not seen at the time of writing this note). Giacomella Orofino has published an excellent English translation (including the root-text and the commentary) of the sixth chapter, dealing with the bardo states, in the last part of her *Sacred Tibetan Teachings on Death and Liberation*. Recently, a complete Italian translation (with a partially nontraditional commentary) has been published by G. Baroetto, in *Il Libro Tibetano dei Sei Lumi*, 2002.

4. Translated with commentary by Jean-Luc Achard, *The Precepts in Eight Chapters*, Zhangzhung Nyengyü Studies, vol. IV.

5. It is said that Dru Gyelwa (1242–90) wrote a commentary on this text but this may be a mistake since such a work has not been found yet. It is also possible that Dru Gyelwa actually composed such a commentary and that it was lost in the course of time. This has to be checked carefully. On the reference to such a commentary, see the *Bon gyi brten 'gyur chen mo*, vol. 154, p. 206.5: *snyan rgyud le'u brgyad pa'i 'grel bru rgyal can* ("...a commentary on the Oral Transmission's *Eight Precepts*, authored by Dru Gyelwa...").

6. The English translation and the commentary of this text were completed years ago in the course of the seminary "Histoire et interprétation des textes et des doctrines" (CNRS, Paris) and will appear in a forthcoming volume.

experience of the natural state (*gnas lugs*), its visionary displays, the manner in which one reaches the Fruit of Buddhahood if one is able to perfect the Path, and the way in which one errs into conditioned existence if one fails to recognize one's real nature in both its abiding and visionary modes. Other themes dealt with in detail are cosmological issues, as well as a general introduction to the bardo states and the death process.

1. THE HISTORICAL SETTING

According to traditional accounts, these teachings were first revealed by Tapihritsa to Gyerpung Nangzher Löpo in the eighth century.[7] In the history of the lineage, Tapihritsa is said to have been a disciple of Tsepung Dawa Gyeltsen,[8] the twenty-fourth lineage holder of a line of transmission in which all masters reached Buddhahood in a single lifetime and manifested the Rainbow Body (*'ja' lus*) at the end of their life. Having received the complete transmission from his master, Tapihritsa decided to practice the secret instructions of Dawa Gyeltsen during solitary retreats in the mountains. After nine years of

---

7. It is rather difficult to prove this assertion since no trace or independent contemporary references to the text (and the cycle it belongs to) seem to appear before the eleventh century. All one can say is that the tradition ascribes the composition of this work (and those making up the *Zhangzhung Nyengyü*, with the exception of the two commentaries on the *Six Lamps*, however) to the two figures mentioned above. Several anachronistic problems have been noted by modern European scholars regarding the history of the *Zhangzhung Nyengyü*. See, for instance, Henk Blezer, "Greatly Perfected in Space and Time."

8. And not *Lawa Gyaltsen as he is recurrently and wrongly named in the various prints and reprints of Tenzin Wangyal's *Wonders of the Natural Mind*. Despite numerous warnings, the translators of the French version have perpetuated this mistake (as well as one about *khyab rig*, etc.).

total immersion in the principles of the teachings, Tapihritsa reached Buddhahood and manifested the "Body of the Great Transfer" (*'pho ba chen po'i sku*), a special modality of the Rainbow Body in which the individual does not manifest death in any way whatsoever but gains power over his entire existence and can manifest as he wants, when he wants, and in the form he wants to choose.[9] Reaching the Rainbow Body would appear as rather "common" compared to this realization of the Great Transfer, since very few individuals are said to have achieved it. Among them are Drenpa Namkha and Tsewang Rigdzin.[10]

Apparently, even if he had already given the full transmission of the teachings of the Great Perfection to Tapihritsa, Tsepung Dawa Gyeltsen revealed them again to a later disciple of his, Gyerpung Nangzher Löpo, in violation of the tradition of transmitting the teaching to a single individual (*gcig brgyud*). One may legitimately wonder if the scheme of the single transmission (*gcig brgyud*) was maintained in these two cases since, most evidently, Dawa Gyeltsen gave the complete transmission to two individuals. Or one might presume that he gave one part to Tapihritsa and another part to Nangzher. However, with the exception of several texts from the first section of the *Zhangzhung Nyengyü*, the texts of the *Kagyü Korzhi* forming the core of the whole cycle are presented as the works of Tapihritsa and Gyerpung, and it is precisely to these and related works that the

---

9. On the four different kinds of Rainbow Bodies, see Achard, *Les Corps d'Arc-en-ciel et leur interprétation selon Düdjom Rinpoche*, Khyung-mkhar 2012, pdf edition.

10. In the Nyingma tradition, masters said to have reached that level are Padmasambhava, Vimalamitra, and the late-eleventh-century figure Chetsün Senge Wangchuk.

notion of "single transmission" applies.[11] In fact, one can only presume that the teachings Dawa Gyeltsen gave Tapihritsa were more or less similar to those contained in the last three sections of the *Zhangzhung Nyengyü*, but given the traditional proto-historical context, it is clearly not the actual contents of these texts that were transmitted then. Lopön Tenzin Namdak is of the opinion that the first part of the *Kagyü Korzhi* existed most probably in a written form before Tapihritsa and that the latter received this section from Dawa Gyeltsen, as well as complementary oral teachings. These oral teachings were then later revealed by Tapihritsa to Nangzher Löpo, forming the three remaining sections of the *Kagyü Korzhi*.

According to the traditional accounts found in the *Zhangzhung Nyengyü* itself, Gyerpung Chenpo handed over the transmission he had received from Tapihritsa to Gyelzik Sechung, when the latter was aged seventy-three. He had previously found out that the best vessel for his transmission was a three-year-old boy named Mu Tsoge (dMu Tsog ge). However, since the child was too young, Gyerpung gave the transmission to Gyelzik Sechung, who was relatively well educated in terms of knowledge and ritual practice. At the time of the transmission, Gyerpung did a retreat lasting five years during which he transmitted the teachings to Gyelzik in a very peculiar way. He had a hole pierced in the wall of his retreat cell and would insert a small straw stalk inside the hole so that the other extremity of the stalk could enter one of Gyelzik's ears. In this way, nobody

---

11. According to modern exegesis, several texts belonging to the first section of the cycle existed prior to Tapihritsa and Nangzher Löpo, whereas most works included in sections 2–4 are the teachings of Tapihritsa transcribed by his disciple Nangzher Löpo.

could possibly hear any word of the transmission. It is reported by the later tradition (exemplified by Patön Tengyel Zangpo, but obviously based on previous works) that Gyelzik reached complete realization when he received the transmission and that he attained full Buddhahood within a year.

After a succession of five more masters, the teachings were transmitted to Pönchen Tsenpo, from whom the lineage divided into two branches. After some time, these two branches were brought back together by Yangtön Sherab Gyeltsen, who played a crucial role in collating the oral teachings of the Experiential Transmission (*Nyams rgyud*) and in the authoring of several complementary works.

The lineage of transmission has remained unbroken down to the present day, with several distinct lines of masters, both in the Eternal Bön (*gyung drung bon*) and in the New Bön (*bon gsar*) traditions.[12]

2. THE TEACHINGS OF THE GREAT PERFECTION

2-1. The *Zhangzhung Nyengyü*

The *Oral Transmission of Zhangzhung* is a very peculiar set of Dzogchen teachings. In the perspective of the practice of the Path, it may well be regarded as entirely sufficient in itself, provided oral instructions (and transmissions) are received from a

---

12. The Menri lineage of the *Zhangzhung Nyengyü* is not the only one that exists, as is usually believed by Western Bönpos. There are several important lineages still active in Tibet as well as in Dolpo. Of course, each of them is introduced by its partisans as the most important one, but one thing that is certain is that the Dolpo lineage goes back to the early Yangtön masters and should therefore be counted as one of the foremost lines of transmission.

qualified lineage holder.[13] As a collection said to trace its origins into the country of Zhangzhung, it does not make use of traditional doxographic schemes such as Mind Series (*Sems sde*), Space Series (*Klong sde*), or Precepts Series (*Man ngag sde*), nor does it use such typical expressions as Trekchö (*khregs chod*) and Thögel (*thod rgal*), despite the presence of the related practices described in some of its texts.[14]

The collection is organized in a set of teachings clearly divided into two complementary corpuses of works:

- the cycle of Secret Formulas (*gsang sngags skor*) and
- the cycle of Dzogchen (*rdzogs chen skor*).[15]

The Secret Formulas or tantric instructions associated with the *Zhangzhung Nyengyü* practice are themselves divided into three main cycles: (1) Secret Formulas (*gsang sngags*), (2) Knowledge Formulas (*rigs sngags*), and (3) what is known as *This-ngak* (*this sngags*), a particular cycle of tantric instructions.[16] What should

---

13. It makes no sense at all to engage the practice of this cycle if one has not received beforehand the required initiations—the *Initiation to the Dynamism of Awareness* (*Rig pa'i rtsal dbang*), the *Great Primordial Initiation* (*Ye dbang chen mo*), and the initiation of the Yidam, Zhangzhung Meri—as well as the direct introduction to the nature of the mind.

14. The expression *thod rgal* that appears in the *Precepts in Twelve Chapters* does not have the same meaning as in the Thögel practice of Dzogchen. It appears in the context of the description of the capacities of individuals: instantaneous (*cig char ba*), direct (*thod rgal ba*), or gradual (*rim gyis/skyes pa*). See also below, p. 14 n. 27.

15. Yangtön Pelzang, *The Extended List containing the Enumeration of works belonging to the Oral Transmission of the Great Perfection in Zhangzhung* (*rDzogs pa chen po zhang zhung snyan rgyud kyi rtsis byang thems yig rgyas pa*), p. 2.

16. The exact meaning of the word *This* seems to have been lost by modern Bönpos. This would require further research.

be remembered is that both Knowledge Formulas and *This* Formulas actually belong to the "precepts" (*man ngag*) of the Secret Formulas. In other words, Secret Formulas have Tantras (*rgyud*), special instructions (*lung*), and precepts (*man ngag*), the last division being composed of the second and third category of tantric Formulas listed above. None of these cycles of instructions has been studied in depth or even basically described yet. The reason might be that it seems very difficult to equate the complex subdivisions of these tantric teachings (as given, for instance, in Yangtön Pelzang's *Extended List*) with actual texts.[17]

The Dzogchen section of the *Zhangzhung Nyengyü* is itself divided into two sets of works:

- the Four Cycles of the Oral Transmission (*bKa' rgyud skor bzhi*), which was transmitted by the Upper lineage (*stod lugs*), and
- the Experiential Transmission (*Nyams rgyud*), which was transmitted by the Lower lineage (*smad lugs*).[18]

The four root-texts forming the core of the Four Cycles of the Oral Transmission have been listed above in the first part of this introduction. These and other complementary texts are dispatched according to the outer, inner, secret, and innermost secret cycles or main divisions of the *Zhangzhung Nyengyü*. It is impossible to state with any temporal certainty when the repartition of these works was undertaken, but upon studying some of the doxographical works included in the Experiential Transmis-

---

17. Yangtön Pelzang, *The Extended List*, p. 3, very laconically says that details should be searched elsewhere.

18. The adjectives Upper and Lower are geographical, not qualitative.

sion, it seems clear that there was not any universal consensus as to which text should be included in which cycle. It seems that the tradition mostly exemplified by the Dru lineage has eventually become the classical reference and that its understanding of the proper way of classifying the texts has become predominant.

However, as one will see in part two of this book, some masters of the Yangtön lineage disagree and propose a different way of classifying these texts. This was recently criticized by Shardza Rinpoche in his *Treasury of Space and Awareness* (*dByings rig mdzod*), in which he established the list as he thinks it should be. He uses convincing arguments based on the following allegorical explanation:[19]

> The outer cycle (*phyi skor*) is similar to the palace of a king, whereas the three other cycles are compared to its treasure house (*mdzod khang*). If one does not enter inside the palace of the king, one will not be able to see its treasure house. In the same way, if one does not perfect the actual meaning of the outer cycle (with the *Precepts in Twelve Chapters* and related works), one will not be able to contemplate the mansion of Wisdom (which is compared to the treasure house of the king). The *Twelve Son-Tantras* and its three ancillary works[20] can then be used to develop a deeper familiarization with the View (*lta ba*).
>
> In order to enter the treasure house, one needs a key to open its entrance door and this very key is symbolized by

---

19. He later confirmed his own approach in a work he has added to the Nyarong version of the *Zhangzhung Nyengyü*. This text was translated in Achard, *La Structure du Zhangzhung Nyengyü*, pp. 35–39.

20. On these texts see ibid., pp. 26–27 (nos. 3–5).

the text of the *Six Lamps* and its ancillary works. Once this door has been opened, one can contemplate the treasures hidden within. In a similar way, owing to the instructions of the inner cycle (*nang skor*) contained in the *Six Lamps*, the visions of Clear-Light can be concretely seen by the practitioner.

At that time, the yogi clearly sees Awareness in its nakedness (*rig pa gcer mthong*), which is the purpose of the *Precepts in Eight Chapters*. The study of this text— the only one included in the secret cycle (*gsang skor*)—is compared to a child seeing the marvels contained in the treasure house but who is still unsure about their overall value. This example indicates that the practitioner might at this stage still be uncertain about the original nature of these visions.[21]

This certainty can be obtained by practicing the principles of the innermost secret cycle (*yang gsang skor*) as contained in the *Twenty-One Seals* and its ancillary works. Its practice leads to the exhaustion of the intellect and phenomena (*blo zad bon zad*) and results in the total realization of the Primordial Purity (*ka dag*) of the natural state.

This way of classifying the texts was followed by Yongdzin Sangye Tendzin Rinpoche when he compiled one of the most recent (and probably the most widely used) versions of the collection.[22]

---

21. This may of course not be the case, since the *Eight Precepts* are more than explicit about the nature of the visions, but the image of uncertainty is used here in order to demonstrate the increasing subtlety within the Four Cycles, as one moves from one to the next.

22. A print of this version was taken by Yongdzin Lopön Tenzin Namdak Rinpoche into exile and was used for the reprint published in *History and Doctrine of Bon*

The second collection of the Dzogchen section of the *Zhangzhung Nyengyü*, known as the Experiential Transmission (*Nyams rgyud*), is a generic designation that applies to three (and to only three) sets of works:

- the extensive version of the Experiential Transmission (*Nyams rgyud rgyas pa*),
- the intermediate version of this Transmission (*Nyams rgyud 'bring po*), and
- the condensed version containing miscellaneous works (*Nyams rgyud bsdus pa thor bu*).[23]

The first one is further divided into two subcycles, known as the Brown Version (*sMug gu*) and the Grey Version (*sKya ru*). They show very similar contents, although the order of the subtexts is not the same in both versions.

The intermediate version contains a set of eight works that should actually be counted as a first, introductory work followed by seven texts with allegorical titles (using similes of the body and its clothes).[24]

---

po Nispanna Yoga in Delhi in 1968. Regarding the story of how Rinpoche secured a copy of the *Zhangzhung Nyengyü* during exile, see Achard, *La Biographie de Lopön Tenzin Namdak Rinpoche*, vol. I, pp. 65–66.

23. It is therefore a dramatic doxographical mistake to classify Dru Gyelwa's *Chaktri* (*Phyag khrid*) as belonging to the Experiential Transmission, as is currently done by several younger Bönpo lamas, despite Yongdzin Rinpoche's recurrent explanations and teachings on this cycle, which he clearly associates with the Oral Transmission, not with the Experiential Transmission. On such a mistake and others, see Achard, "Mesmerizing with the Useless?"

24. The meaning of these titles is explained by Shardza Rinpoche in the first volume of his *Treasury of Space and Awareness* (*dByings rig mdzod*, vol. I, pp. 62–63). In this section of Shardza Rinpoche's work, what should be counted as "Experiential

The condensed version is certainly the most interesting of the entire Experiential Transmission in terms of actual yogic instructions for practice. It contains explicit precepts dealing with Thögel meditation (although the term *Thögel* is not used) and extensive instructions on dark retreats (*mun mtshams*). What is clear is that this condensed version is not a kind of summary of the two preceding cycles (as its title might suggest), but rather a collection containing extra material that was not included in the extensive and intermediate versions. For instance, it contains a long series of "single transmission" (*gcig rgyud*) texts that are not to be found elsewhere in the cycles of the Experiential Transmission or the collection of the Four Cycles. These texts are of great relevance for the practice of the Six Lamps.

2-2. The nature of the Base, Awareness, and Mind

In the first chapter of the *Instructions on the Six Lamps*, one will read a very clear and simple explanation of what are known as the Universal Base (*kun gzhi*), Awareness (*rig pa*), and mind (*sems* or *blo*).[25] The Base is designated as such because it is the very ground that can become the Base of Saṃsāra or the Base of Nirvāṇa, depending upon the realization or nonrealization of the nature of its manifestations (*gzhi snang*).

This Base is the true essence of one's mind, abiding as the union of Emptiness and Clarity (*stong gsal*). The knowledge of this Base is called *Rigpa* (*rig pa*), a totally discerning Awareness that is independent from discursive thoughts (but also not

Transmission" is clearly delineated and de facto excludes the *Chaktri* from this category of texts.

25. Throughout the cycle, *sems* (mind), *blo* (intellect), and *yid* (mental) are used interchangeably, even if their respective connotations are maintained when necessary.

impeded by the arising of thoughts), which "knows" its true nature as being the Absolute Body (*bon sku*).[26]

The nature of one's Awareness is such that it abides in its essence (*ngo bo*) as a totally clear and unimpeded transparency, naked and luminous. In its Primordial Purity, it thus abides as a discerning knowledge that has no object except itself. Being free from and not obstructed by the movements characterizing discursiveness, it simply arises primordially in a nongrasping mode.

As to mind (*sems*), it is simply the discursive process of dualistic grasping based on ignorance (*ma rig pa*). Its functions are mainly dualistic and analytical. Reifying this mind as the sole abiding mode of one's real nature is the perpetuation of delusion and ignorance. In fact, one can define mind as functioning according to a mode of ignorance (*ma rig pa'i tshul*), while the nature of the Mind (*sems nyid*) abides in the mode of one's discerning Awareness (*rig pa'i tshul*). When one abides in the mode of ignorance, one remains in conditioned existence and the Base abides as a base of delusion (*'khrul gzhi*). On the contrary, when one abides in the mode of Awareness, one remains in the recognition of one's natural state and the Base abides as a Base of Liberation (*grol gzhi*).

Therefore, since time immemorial, one has failed to recognize one's own nature. For this reason, the manifestations of the Base have been apprehended as objects manifesting from a source other than oneself (*gzhan snang*), causing one to enter the path of delusion. To regain knowledge of one's natural state and avoid the wandering into the pits of saṃsāric existence, one

26. On the key identification of Awareness (*rig pa*) and the Absolute Body (*bon sku*), see Achard, *The Precepts in Eight Chapters*, in which explanations are introduced on this theme, based on the traditional texts of the lineage.

should engage in the special practice of Dzogchen, starting with the correct understanding and experience of one's own Awareness through Trekchö practice. The corresponding teachings in the *Six Lamps* are described in the first two Lamps as well as in chapters III and IV of Dru Gyelwa's *Chaktri* and the first chapters of the *Twenty-One Seals*.

Basically, the practice consists in remaining in the fivefold position, facing a deep blue sky, and breathing normally without blockage. Concentrating without tension on the outer sky, after a few days, one will experience the "separation of the pure from the impure" (*dwangs snyigs dbye ba*) in which Awareness dawns spontaneously without being conditioned by anything. When one reaches a sufficient stabilization of the experience of Awareness through this practice, one should then cultivate it without artifice and integrate it to the key points (*gnad*) of Thögel practice described in the following section.

2-3. Instructions on visionary practice

The main practice of Dzogchen is concerned with stabilizing the experience of the natural state and contemplating its dynamic manifestations in ever increasing visions. These two aspects of the practice are generally known as Trekchö (*khregs chod*, Cutting through Rigidity) and Thögel (*thod rgal*, Passing over the Crest). These two words are not used in the *Zhangzhung Nyengyü* corpus, except for Thögel but not with the meaning intended here.[27] However, their actual practice is of course

---

27. As mentioned above in note 14, it is used in the context of the gradation of capacities among practitioners. These are generally classified as gradualists (*rim gyis pa, rim skyes pa*), those able to skip stages (*thod rgal ba*), and instantaneists (*cig char ba*). This classification occurs in the *Precepts in Twelve Chapters* (*Man ngag le'u bcu gnyis pa*) of the outer section of the *Zhangzhung Nyengyü*. There, it is said

explained in the practice manuals of the *Zhangzhung Nyengyü*,
such as the *Chaktri* (*Phyag khrid*) of Dru Gyelwa Yungdrung
(1242–90).[28] In this context the literal understanding of the
two expressions appears clearly meaningful as it delineates the
correct approach to the practice; it is thus generally said: "If
the rigidity has not been cut, then the crest will not be passed
over" (*khregs ma chod na/ thod mi rgal ba/*). This means that
if the rigidity of the conditioned mind is not eradicated, then
the actual core of the visionary practice of Dzogchen will not
be enabled. But it also means more: it means that Thögel practice must be performed within the actual experience of Trekchö.
This entails that after an initial familiarization with Trekchö
alone (in order to stabilize the experience of the natural state),
Thögel should be practiced within the actual experience of the
natural state (through Trekchö).[29]

The instructions about Thögel practice are not ordinary ones
and should not be taught to an unworthy or unqualified vessel.
In the last chapter of his *Chaktri*, Dru Gyelwa says that a proper
vessel should be:

> that practitioners of lower capacities are guided in a gradual mode; those of inter-
> mediate capacities enabling them to skip stages are guided through the direct
> revelation of the essence of Wisdom; and those of instantaneous realization are
> simply taught the nondifferentiation of appearances and mind (*snang sems dbyer
> med*). See *Man ngag leu' bcu gnyis pa*, pp. 117–19.

28. See Lopön Tenzin Namdak (ed. Gerd Manusch), *The Main Dzogchen Practices*
and *The Meditation on the Clear-Light* (see bibliography for full references, under
Yongdzin Rinpoche). Kurt Keutzer has also prepared translations of the entire
manual of Dru Gyelwa's *Chaktri*, including the Tibetan text (see the bibliography
for complete references).

29. In other words, after an initial familiarization with Trekchö alone, Trekchö and
Thögel should be practiced together.

...A person endowed with good karma and (spiritual) fortune, mainly concerned with the next life,[30] (possessing) diligence and great generosity; his faith and devotion should be associated with (a natural) compassion; he should gather assiduity and determination, practice austerity and endurance, be flexible in terms of thoughts and actions,[31] be endowed with mindfulness and vigilance, be of proper (health in terms of his) elements, and be in the prime of life.[32]

Therefore, to such a rare chalice, the qualified master should teach the principles of Thögel without hiding anything or holding back any instructions. The most extensive explanations

---

30. John Reynolds (*The Practice of Dzogchen...*, p. 192) understands *phyi ma la gtso bor 'dzin pa* as "should subsequently be kept as the principal (disciple)." This is wrong. *Phyi ma la* has no adverbial function here and simply means "about the next life," a classical idiom frequently found in traditional texts. Furthermore, *gtso bor 'dzin pa* does not mean "to be kept as the principal" but rather "to be mostly concerned with."

31. This was not correctly understood in Reynolds (ibid.), who translates "who is suitable in all his actions according to plan." The text has: *bsam sbyor las su rung ba. bSam sbyor* refers to thoughts and actions, to what one thinks and how one acts. *Las su rung ba* has several meanings, such as "acceptable," "proper," sometimes also "brought under control," which could work here too. I have chosen "flexible" because it implies that the person described perfectly controls his mind and his actions and is able to manage them in a workable manner.

32. This was also clearly not understood in Reynolds (ibid.), where it is translated as "who can spread and abide in what is proper." This rendering does not mean anything. The text is however very clear; it says: *'byung rung dar la bab*. Reynolds has taken *dar* to mean "spread," but here it refers to a young adult, and the classical expression *dar la bab* means "in the prime of life" and not "spread." Furthermore, *'byung rung* has nothing to do with "to abide in what is proper" but refers to the fact that the practitioner should be healthy and endowed with proper (*rung*), equilibrated elements (*'byung*).

about the practice of Thögel in Bön texts are included in three chapters of Shardza Rinpoche's *Treasury of Space and Awareness* (chaps. 15–17). The first describes generalities about Thögel, the second deals with the actual practice itself, and the third is entirely dedicated to dark retreats (*mun mtshams*).

Thus in chapter 15 of the *Treasury of Space and Awareness*, one is first introduced to the ten superiorities of Thögel over Trekchö.[33] These cover subjects such as superiorities in terms of purification of dualistic grasping, purification of consciousness, visions of Clear-Light, stages and paths, etc. Then the author describes in a general way some of the key points of Thögel practice, including the four Channels of Light (*'od rtsa bzhi*) and the Four Visions (*snang ba bzhi*), and gives a lengthy explanation of the Four Lamps (*sgron ma bzhi*), as well as several other peculiar elements belonging to Thögel practice such as the visionary manifestations of the Three Bodies along the Path, the eternal chains of Awareness (*rig pa g.yung drung lu gu rgyud*), etc.

In the next chapter, the author starts with a detailed description of the key points of body, speech, and mind. The body should be placed in one of the five main postures that are described in the manuals of the *Zhangzhung Nyengyü*, namely the positions of the Lion (*seng ge*), the Elephant (*glang chen*), the Sage (*dge sbyor*), the Swan (*ngang mo*), and the Antelope (*gna' pho*). Using these postures is decisive insofar as Wisdom abides within the body. Thus, if the body is not controlled through the use of these postures, then the natural radiance of Awareness will not be seen

---

33. Usually only seven are discussed in Nyingma works. This is therefore one particularity of Bönpo Dzogchen teachings: to explain these superiorities with a number of ten modalities.

during Contemplation. As to speech, the voice should remain silent and breathing should be performed through the mouth. As to the mind, it should be focused on the eyes and these fixed on visionary Space (*dbyings*).

Following this (and still in the same chapter), the author describes at length the next four key points (*gnad bzhi*), namely those of (1) doorways, (2) objects, (3) breath, and (4) Awareness. The key point of doorways concerns the orientation of the gazes used during the practice and corresponding to the posture one is using. The objects are the supports (*rten*) of practice such as the sky, the rays of the sun, the moon, butter lamps, and the darkness of a special cell (*mun khang*). As to the key point of breath, the air should go through the mouth, with equal inhalations and exhalations. A slight holding of the breath with empty lungs should also be performed. Shardza Rinpoche says that without this key point, anyone training in Thögel will not see the visions of the natural state. As to the key point of Awareness, there are up to six elements to take into account: View (*lta ba*), Meditation (*sgom pa*), Conduct (*spyod pa*), the three natural radiances (*rang bzhin gyi gdangs gsum*),[34] the four clarities (*gsal ba bzhi*),[35]

---

34. These are the natural radiance of the pure sky, the natural radiance of the pure Reality, and the luminous radiance of pure Wisdom. The first is simply the celestial purity of the sky that is free from characteristics. The second is the Awareness of the Path (*lam gyi rig pa*) realizing the empty transparency of the Awareness of the Base (*gzhi'i rig pa*), both fusing like the sky mixing with the sky. The third refers to the visions of Wisdom that arise as the natural displays of fivefold lights, Thiglés, etc. (*dByings rig mdzod*, II, pp. 270–71).

35. These are (1) the clarity of the senses (*dbang po*) whose doorways are not obstructed by anything; (2) the clarity of the mind that is not covered by the five poisons; (3) the clarity of consciousness that is not soiled by dualistic grasping; and (4) the clarity of the intellect that is free from the tempests of discursiveness. The source of these four clarities is said to be the *Yetri Thasel*, which is quoted in the *Treasury of Space and Awareness* (II, p. 272). However,

and an explanation of how visions arise from the natural state itself.

This latter theme is the perfect link for the next section of this chapter, which is concerned with the detailed explanation of the Four Visions (*snang ba bzhi*), the scheme in Five Visions (*snang ba lnga*) peculiar to the *Zhangzhung Nyengyü* being discussed in the context of dark retreats (*mun mtshams*).

In conclusion to this chapter, Shardza Rinpoche describes the four final precepts, which contain, among other things, explanations about the signs occurring during the practice, etc. These signs are of tremendous importance in order to clearly identify the stage one has reached in the course of the practice itself.

Dark retreats are one of the main practices performed in Dzogchen teachings.[36] They exist in different forms or supports and are practiced either before daylight Thögel or after, depending on the cycle one practices. For instance, in the *Zhangzhung Nyengyü*, these retreats are performed before daylight Thögel, whereas in cycles such as the *Refined Gold of the Great Perfection* (*rDzogs chen gser zhun*), they are performed afterward.

Generally speaking, these retreats are given in "Black Guidance" (*nag khrid*) kind of instructions, but there also exists (in New Bön and the Nyingma tradition) a special kind of dark retreat called "Variegated Guidance" (*khra khrid*), which demands a special cell with openings on the four walls.[37] In a

so far, I haven't been able to locate that quote in the *Yetri* cycle itself.

36. There are also dark retreats in the context of the *Kālacakratantra* but they do not lead to visionary developments similar to those of Dzogchen. On this subject, the third Dodrupchen Rinpoche explains the difference between the two. See Tony Duff, *About the Three Lines that Strike Key Points*, pp. 24–25.

37. Yongdzin Rinpoche confirms (private meeting, Shenten Ling, 2006) that such Variegated Guidance does not exist within the teachings of Eternal Bön. Indeed,

certain sense, retreats based on this Variegated Guidance are the core of Dzogchen teachings, combining daylight Thögel and dark retreats proper. With the exception of this Variegated Guidance, dark retreats, which are performed for the duration of at least seven weeks, can be of the following kinds:

- dark retreats using mostly *Tsalung* (*rtsa rlung*) kind of techniques like in the *Seven Cycles of Clear-Light* (*'Od gsal bdun skor*) of the *Zhangzhung Nyengyü*;
- dark retreats using mostly Peaceful and Wrathful Deities (*zhi khro*) like those found in the *Yangtse Longchen* or in the *Kusum Rangshar*; and
- dark retreats based on two specific yogic instructions known as "Pressing the Ocean" (*rgya mtsho ar la gtad pa*) and "Entering the Glow of the Ocean" (*rgya mtsho dwangs su zhugs pa*).

In the system of the *Zhangzhung Nyengyü*, by indulging in the practice of dark retreats again and again, the yogi will gradually experience five successive visionary stages forming the Five Visions (*snang ba lnga*) mentioned previously and listed as:

- the Increasing of Visions (*snang ba 'phel ba*),
- the Spreading of Visions (*snang ba mched pa*),
- the Intensification of Visions (*snang ba rgyas pa*),
- the Perfection of Visions (*snang ba rdzogs pa*), and
- the Ultimate Stage of Visions (*snang ba mthar thug*).

---

so far, I have found references to such retreats only in the Nyingma and New Bön traditions.

If the practitioner is able to perfect all five visionary stages, then he is certain to reach Buddhahood in his lifetime and to manifest the Rainbow Body (*'ja' lus*) at the end of his life. If he fails to perfect all those stages and does not reach enlightenment before death, he will be confronted with the intermediate states (bardos) arising after his demise.

2-4. The arising of intermediate states

The Lamp of the Moment of the Bardo (*bar do dus kyi sgron ma*) mentions explicitly only two kinds of bardos but obviously refers to a third one, given the contents of this Lamp. The two bardos that are mentioned by name are (1) the Bardo of the Clear-Light of Reality (*bon nyid 'od gsal gyi bar do*) and (2) the Bardo of Becoming (*srid pa'i bar do*). It however clearly refers to the Bardo of the Time of Death (*'chi ka'i bar do*), since it extensively describes the moment when body and mind separate. In the *Chaktri*, Dru Gyelwa describes three bardo states in the chapter on Conduct (*spyod pa*). He mentions the Bardo of the Abiding Base (*gnas pa gzhi bar do*), as well as the Bardo of the Clear-Light of Reality and the Empty Bardo of Becoming (*stong pa srid pa'i bar do*). From its description, the Bardo of the Abiding Base appears as identical to the Bardo of the Primordially Pure Absolute Body (*ka dag bon sku'i bar do*), which is rarely discussed in the sources at our disposal. Most Tibetan schools consider it as a blank or dark state without consciousness. It is on the contrary described in Dzogchen teachings as the state in which one is directly in the experience of the Absolute Body (*bon sku*). However, it is also said to last as long as one is able to remain undistracted in the experience of the natural state. This means that ordinary beings and nonadvanced practitioners have no actual possibility to recognize it.

After its extensive description of the dissolutions of the elements and their winds at the time of death, the text describes the mode of liberation (*grol tshul*) of the three main categories of practitioners: superior, medium, and lower ones.

Those of superior capacities reach enlightenment in this very life and do not have to pass through the narrow path of the bardos.

Those of medium capacities may reach enlightenment after the disconnection of the mind and the body, but they need to have been deeply familiar with their natural state during their lifetime in order to reach Buddhahood at that time. If their recognition of Awareness is not impeded by the experience of death, they will see the natural arising of the Three Bodies at the time of the Bardo of Clear-Light and will reach enlightenment without further delay.

Practitioners of lower capacities are generally unable to recognize the Bardo of the Clear-Light of Reality and are thus propelled into the Bardo of Becoming by their own karma. For some, it might still be possible to perform a postmortem Phowa (*'pho ba*) at that time, provided sufficient training in this practice has been obtained during the lifetime and provided they can recognize their situation as being that of the bardo, remember the instructions, etc. After successfully performing this Phowa, they will gain a fortunate rebirth in a pure realm and will reach liberation after this ultimate rebirth.

Ordinary individuals are helplessly drawn by their karma toward a new matrix and will have to take rebirth according to their past actions. Erring in the six destinies, it will require a tremendous amount of good karma to regain a human rebirth and to engage in the practice of the teachings of Eternal Bön. Generally, given the negative nature of their karma, ordinary individuals wander endlessly in the cities of the six destinies without refuge. Their situation rarely provides, if ever, favorable circumstances to gather good karma. For this reason, at the end of this Lamp, Tapihritsa exhorts Nangzher Löpo (and through him all practitioners of this cycle) to seriously think about the flaws of delusion and to give up saṃsāric expectations. The time allowed by our karma to keep that human rebirth is more than uncertain and for this reason one should welcome all opportunities to practice with zeal during serious retreats.

2-5. Instructions on the nature of the Fruit

There is no explicit discussion of the nature of the Fruit (*'bras bu*) in the root-text itself but it might certainly be enlightening to discuss the result of the Path in the larger context of Dzogchen teachings. There are, for instance, amazing presentations of the Fruit in Shardza Rinpoche's *Treasury of Space and Awareness* (*dByings rig mdzod*), as well as in his Fruit chapter within the *Natural Arising of the Three Bodies* (*sKu gsum rang shar*).[38] Dru Gyelwa has also authored a text associated with the *Zhangzhung Nyengyü* cycle, entitled *Gradual Instructions on the Decisive Elucidation of the Three Bodies and the Taking Hold of the Natural State of the Fruit* (*'Bras bu rang sa bzung zhing sku gsum dmar thag gcod pa'i khrid rim*), from which we shall briefly summarize the following data:

After two initial sections dedicated to examples and direct introductions to the natural arising (*rang shar*) and natural manifestations (*rang snang*) of sounds, lights, and rays, Dru

---

38. *The Union of Saṃsāra and Nirvāṇa, Instructions on Apprehending the Natural State of the Fruit* (*'Bras bu rang sar bzung ba'i khrid 'khor 'das mnyam sbyor, sKu gsum rang shar*, pp. 153–170).

Gyelwa's text discusses the Fruit in terms of the existence of Buddhahood within oneself and the arising of Bodies (*sku*) and Wisdoms (*ye shes*).

Regarding the natural existence of Buddhahood within oneself,[39] one's Awareness existing within the sanctuary of the Brown Cornelian Tent is the Absolute Body existing naturally within oneself (*bon sku rang chas*). The natural dynamism (*rang rtsal*) of Awareness arising and being totally perfect within the pathway of the channels is the Perfection Body existing naturally within oneself (*rdzogs sku rang chas*). The spiritual marvels that arise at the doorway of the Lamps are the Emanation Body naturally existing within oneself (*sprul sku rang chas*). On this theme, the root-text of the *Twenty-One Seals* says:

> The Absolute Body, which is Self-Awareness, emerges
>   from the expanse of the heart;
> The Body of natural Perfection stands in the pathway of
>   the channels, and
> The Emanation Body emerges naturally at the doorway
>   of the Lamps.

In this perspective, the empty essence of Mind itself (*sems nyid*) corresponds to the natural existence of the Absolute Body within oneself. Its perfect Clarity corresponds to the Perfection Body, and its capacity to manifest itself in an infinite variety of visionary marvels corresponds to its aspect as Emanation Body.[40]

---

39. This subject is dealt with in detail in Achard, *The Precepts in Eight Chapters*.

40. Dru Gyelwa's explanation about Bodies and Wisdoms further describes the Three Bodies in terms of their nature abiding as the three Bodies of the Base (*gzhi'i sku gsum*, corresponding to their natural abiding within oneself, as described above),

At this level of the Fruit, the natural state retains its spontaneous dynamism (*rtsal*) expressed in sounds, lights, and rays. At
that time one understands (and directly experiences) them as
one's natural visions (*rang snang*) displayed and liberated within
the Essence of Awareness (*rig pa'i ngo bo*). In fact, when one
has reached this level of realization, the five-colored lights that
abide as one's fundamental, luminous nature manifest according
to their own characteristics. Thus:

- the white light appears as Künnang Khyabpa in the
  central direction, in union with his *yum*, the goddess of
  the sky element;
- the yellow light appears as Selwa Rangjung in the east-
  ern direction, in union with his *yum*, the goddess of
  the earth element;
- the green light appears as Gelha Garchuk in the north-
  ern direction, in union with his *yum*, the goddess of
  the air element;
- the red light appears as Jedrak Ngömé in the western
  direction, in union with his *yum*, the goddess of the
  fire element; and
- the blue light appears as Gawa Döndrup in the south-
  ern direction, in union with his *yum*, the goddess of
  the water element.

---

the three Bodies of the Path (*lam gyi sku gsum*, namely the actual experience of
these Bodies during the practice of the Path and their arising within one's continuum), and the three Bodies of the Fruit (*'bras bu'i sku gsum*, corresponding to
their concrete arising in their total perfection). I will deal with these three aspects
in detail in a forthcoming short work provisionally entitled *The Three Bodies of
the Great Perfection and Their Expression According to the Base, Path, and Fruit.*

All those deities appear in a mode that is characteristic of that of a central deity surrounded by an entourage. All of these also appear according to outer, inner, and secret forms. They are of a single essence, which manifests itself in one of these three kinds of forms according to the beings to be converted.

Furthermore, the eight associations of consciousnesses (*tshogs brgyad*) manifest as the Eight Primordial Shens (*ye gshen brgyad*)[41] that, with other manifestations such as the five immaculate deities, the six subduing Shens, the four Queens, etc., form the complex group of the forty-five main peaceful deities of the body, etc. In fact, there are forty-five inner peaceful deities and eighty-six wrathful secret manifestations of male and female deities, abiding as a complete maṇḍala.

The fact that these deities appear as couples in union (*yab yum*) is a symbol illustrating the union of Methods and Knowledge, of Clarity and Emptiness, etc. The fact that they appear as a central couple and its entourage in union symbolizes the capacity of liberating the mind and its mental events. Further explanations are given by Dru Gyelwa regarding their manifestations in outer, inner, and secret modes; their activities; the fact that they are endowed with the fivefold set of Body, Speech, Mind, Qualities, and Activities; etc.

The Wisdoms that form the display of Awareness are the five traditional Wisdoms (*ye shes lnga*) that can be subsumed to (1) the ultimate Knowledge realizing things as they are and (2) the relative Knowledge realizing the diversity in which they appear.[42] In general, and as stated by Shardza

---

41. On these and those mentioned hereafter, see Achard, *The Precepts in Eight Chapters*, pp. 105ff.

42. The discussion of Wisdoms in the context of the Fruit is not very detailed in

Rinpoche in his *Treasury of Space and Awareness*, the actual meaning of "Wisdom" (*ye shes*) is "to know clearly the principle of primordial Thusness" (*ye ci bzhin ma yi don gsal bar shes pa*).

These Wisdoms arise as the natural glow (*rang mdangs*) of one's visionary Space (*dbyings*) in a variety of modes that are all insubstantial. Because of their visionary nature, it is also important to differentiate between these Wisdoms themselves and their specific lights (*'od*). The difference between the two is that of gold and the yellow color. Wisdoms also have a sapiential aspect that is the quintessence of Sublime Knowledge (*shes rab snying po*), namely Awareness itself (*rig pa*). Therefore, the relationship between Space (characterized below as empty), Wisdoms, and their sapiential aspect is defined as follows in the *Tantra of the Initiation to the Dynamism of Awareness* (*Rig pa rtsal dbang gi tantra*):

> The empty (Space) is endowed with the quintessence of
> Wisdom (*ye shes*),
> Wisdom is endowed with the quintessence of Knowl-
> edge (*shes rab*), and
> Knowledge is endowed with the quintessence of Aware-
> ness (*rig pa*).

Further explanations given by Shardza Rinpoche in his *Treasury of Space and Awareness* entail a detailed discussion of the three kinds of Wisdoms, namely:

Dru Gyelwa's text. The rest of the discussion given here is based on Shardza Rinpoche's *Treasury of Space and Awareness*.

- the three Wisdoms of the Absolute Body (Essence, Nature, and Compassion),
- the five Wisdoms of the Perfection Body (Wisdom of Emptiness, Mirror-Like Wisdom, etc.), and
- the two Wisdoms of the Emanation Body (Knowledge of the ultimate nature and Knowledge of the relative nature).

Of course, to counteract the functions and activities of the 84,000 passions of deluded individuals, Wisdoms can be multiplied in as many varieties and modalities as necessary, in an increasing mode whose full meaning is that Bodies and Wisdoms are combined together in order to concretely work for the benefit of sentient beings through specific activities.

At the base of these activities are three elements of crucial importance: (1) a great compassion, (2) a perfect skill in liberating means, and (3) omniscience. Through the power of a compassion that is equal for all, unceasing and inexhaustible, one performs the benefit of migrating beings. Through the skill in liberating means, one is able to guide beings by performing specific activities such as appeasing, increasing, etc., or any kind of specific activity required for subjugating beings. And through the marvels of omniscience, one displays the knowledge of the natural state without anything likely to remain hidden from one's understanding, without anything left unclear, etc. These activities are performed on a continuous basis without interruption. No effort is required for their performance since they are done in total, spontaneous perfection. Such altruistic capacities are the concrete result of the aspiration to help all sentient beings formulated at the beginning of the Path, when one first entered the doorway of the teachings of Eternal Bön.

2-6. The way to perform the practice

The actual method for practicing the *Instructions on the Six Lamps* is given in the *Six Essential Points of Pure and Perfect Mind*, which goes back to Orgom Kündül (eleventh century) and Dampa Bumjé (eleventh century), the eldest son of Yangtön Sherab Gyeltsen.[43] The *Six Essential Points* is one of the few manuals of the *Zhangzhung Nyengyü*, and its structure and contents have certainly inspired Dru Gyelwa Yungdrung when he started to compile materials for the redaction of his *Chaktri (Phyag khrid)*.[44] However, in order to perform the practice of the Six Lamps, one first needs to complete the preliminaries (*sngon 'gro*) of the *Zhangzhung Nyengyü* that are described in the *Stages of the Nine [Preliminary] Practices of Bön (Bon spyod dgu rim)*.[45] The nine preliminaries to perform 100,000 times each are (1) practicing self-initiation, (2) meditating on impermanence, (3) confessing bad deeds, (4) generating the enlightened mind, (5) taking refuge, (6) offering the maṇḍala,

---

43. The English translation of this text is forthcoming. See also below n. 54.

44. On the various practice manuals of the *Zhangzhung Nyengyü*, see Achard: "Mesmerizing with the Useless?," pp. 135–37. Some research is necessary to determine whether Dru Gyelwa's work is actually based on the *Zhangtri (Zhang khrid)* compiled by Zhangtön Tsültrim Loden (see Kvaerne, "The Canon of the Tibetan Bonpos," II, no. T 265) or not.

45. A very precise and literal translation of this work has been done by David Germano in *The Experiential* (sic) *Transmission of Drugyelwa Yungdrung, Part One*. Since that time, several translations of this fundamental text for preliminary practices have appeared in various forms and languages. To my knowledge, another version is being prepared by Kurt Keutzer.

(7) purifying one's obscurations, (8) offering one's body,[46] and (9) reciting the prayer to the lineage.[47]

Of course, in the traditional context of the practice of the *Zhangzhung Nyengyü*, one is also expected to perform the outer and inner *Rushen* (*phyi nang ru shan*) as forming the special preliminaries of Dzogchen.[48] These *Rushen* practices do not appear in Dru Gyelwa's *Chaktri* set of teachings. There are two possible reasons for that: (1) these teachings were considered to be highly esoteric and only given orally (until they were eventually put into written form, at least for the inner *Rushen*);[49] or (2) they were included in the curriculum of practices at a later date and were not considered part of the original set of practices.

There are also several initiations that one needs to receive before engaging in the formal practices of this cycle, starting with the initiation to the Yidam practice of Zhangzhung Meri

---

46. This refers to a very simple form of daily *Chö* (*gCod*) practice, slightly simplified compared to the extensive *Chö* practice performed at dusk.

47. Relative to the instructions on how to perform these preliminaries, see Achard, *The Dawn of Awareness*, pp. 21–39. The sole existence of that thirteenth-century text by Dru Gyelwa contradicts the assertions spread by some uneducated individuals within the Western Bönpo and Nyingma communities regarding the fact that preliminaries (*sngon 'gro*) were coined together at a very late date (nineteenth century!) and that they have been imposed as a compulsory set of practices for Westerners. These assertions are utter nonsense.

48. They are also described in *The Dawn of Awareness*, pp. 48–87.

49. There are no "outer *Rushen*" texts or instructions in the entire set of works of the *Zhangzhung Nyengyü* and *Nyamgyü*. However, there is one work (included both in the *Nyengyü* and in the *Nyamgyü*) describing in detail the practice of the inner *Rushen*, and there also exists a related prayer that is to be sung at the end of the sessions of practice (this prayer is included in the *Nyamgyü* only, but it clearly does not belong to it but rather to general works associated with the collection and included in the collection by modern editors).

and to the Protectors practice centered on Gyelpo Nyipangse and Menmo. At the same time, one should receive the instructions on how to perform the *Absolute Activities of Kuntuzangpo* (*Kun bzang don gyi phrin las*), which can be used either for daily *sādhana* practice or as a feast offering (*tsok, ganacakra*).[50]

Then one must receive the two "Dzogchen" initiations associated with this cycle, namely the *Tantra of the Initiation to the Dynamism of Awareness* (*Rig pa'i rtsal dbang gyi tan tra*) and the *Great Primordial Initiation* (*Ye dbang chen mo*) either in its *Terma* (*gter ma*) version or according to that compiled by Shardza Rinpoche. Obviously the transmission of the *lung* (reading transmission) of the text of the *Six Lamps* combined with oral instructions is also compulsory.

According to all senior official lineage holders of the *Zhang-zhung Nyengyü*, it would not make any sense to start the practice of this text without the above-listed prerequisites (in particular without receiving beforehand one of the two initiations mentioned in the previous paragraph).

As explained by Yongdzin Rinpoche, the practice can be performed in a nonelaborate manner (*spros med tshul*) or in an elaborate manner (*spros bcas tshul*). The nonelaborate approach concerns only highly advanced practitioners who remain in the contemplation of their visionary nature without interruption and who thus continuously abide in what is known as the Horizon of Day and Night (*nyin mtshan 'khor yug*). This means

---

50. Explanation and transmission courtesy of Yongdzin Rinpoche. Except for the French translation used at the Khyung-mkhar Association, I don't know of any other translations of this text that is of crucial importance for the daily practice of the *Zhangzhung Nyengyü*. Parts of the *sādhana* practice included in this text are used or referred to in Shardza Rinpoche's compilation of *The Great Primordial Initiation* (*Ye dbang chen mo*).

that they practice constantly, being entirely focused (without breaks) on the visions of Thögel, including during their dreams. Such a level can be achieved only after years and years of intensive retreats and is in no way among the possibilities of ordinary practitioners.

The elaborate approach is based on a daily program covering most practices performed on the Path of Bön. This entails performing on a daily basis the tantric practices (including *Tsok* offering) as they are found in the activity manual of the *Zhangzhung Nyengyü* (the *Absolute Activities of Kuntuzangpo*), as well as the Zhangzhung Meri *sādhana* and the invocations of the two Guardians of the teachings: Gyelpo Nyipangse and Menmo. Obviously this program includes the performance of the four daily offerings: fumigations (*bsang*) in the morning, water offering (*chu gtor*) before noon, burnt food (*gsur*) in the late afternoon, and *Chö* (*gCod*) after sunset. One should also follow the actual order of practices as they have been established, for instance, by Dru Gyelwa in his *Chaktri* manual. Yongdzin Rinpoche has written a detailed program for retreats, which can also be followed by serious practitioners. This program is of great help for understanding how to actually progress along the Path of Dzogchen, without many obstacles and with a great celerity. This text is not included in his *Collected Works*. It was written by Rinpoche during the winter of 1998–99 in Triten Norbutsé and consists of five pages, its title being the *Succession of Practices for the Dzogchen Training* (*rDzogs chen khrid sbyong phyag len gyi go rim*). Translations in both French and English have been published by the Khyung-mkhar Association.

3. THE TEXT OF THE *SIX LAMPS*

The text of the *Six Lamps* comes with a set of other works, four of which are intimately associated with it, two of these being direct commentaries written by medieval masters of the lineage.[51]

The first is the *Ornament of Solar Lights*, a commentary composed by Uri Sönam Gyeltsen (thirteenth century),[52] which just preceded the second work, the *Commentary on the Contemplative Meaning of the Six Lamps*, a composition by Dru Gyelwa Yungdrung (1242–90).[53]

The third work is the short practice manual known as the *Six Essential Points of Pure and Perfect Mind* (*Byang chub sems kyi gnad drug*), which explains the practice of the *Six Lamps*.[54] According to the tradition, this manual is attributed to Yangtön Sherab Gyeltsen, but the inner evidence found in

---

51. We will see below in part two another way of classifying and describing the works surrounding the *Six Lamps*.

52. The full title is *The Ornament of Solar Lights: A Commentary on the Lamps Extracted from the Oral Transmission of the Great Perfection in Zhangzhung* (*rDzogs pa chen po zhang zhung snyan rgyud las sgron ma'i 'grel nyi 'od rgyan*, Gangs ti se bon gzhung, vol. 24, pp. 264–305). Strangely enough, in his *List Enumerating [the Texts] of the Zhangzhung Nyengyü* (*rDzogs pa chen po zhang zhung snyan rgyud kyi rtsis byang*), Yangtön Pelzang attributes the redaction of this work to Nyagtön Ripa Shertsül (Sherab Tsültrim) instead of the latter's disciple, Uri Sönam Gyeltsen. This was also noted by Henk Blezer ("Greatly Perfected, in Space and Time," p. 92).

53. The full title of this work is *The Commentary on the Contemplative Meaning of the Six Lamps Extracted from the Oral Transmission of the Great Perfection in Zhangzhung* (*rDzogs pa chen po zhang zhung snyan rgyud las sgron ma drug gi dgongs don 'grel pa*, Gangs ti se bon gzhung, rTse zhig dgon, vol. 24, pp. 217–63).

54. A translation and exhaustive commentary of the practice has been published in Achard, *La Pratique des Six Points Essentiels de l'Esprit de Parfaite Pureté*, volume I, Editions Khyung-Lung, 2007. A second volume of instructions is in preparation.

the Experiential Transmission (*Nyams rgyud*), in particular in the medium-size collection, definitely proves that the teachings were actually compiled by his son, Dampa Bumje Ö.

The fourth work is the amazing short treatise known as the *Six Thiglés* (*Thig le drug pa*), which is considered an offshoot of the *Six Lamps* but which brings forth a number of interesting clarifications that are necessary to embrace the full meaning of the root-text itself (i.e., the *Six Lamps*).[55]

The other works belonging to the second division of the *Zhangzhung Nyengyü* pick up specific themes from the *Six Lamps* such as, for example, instructions on the correct understanding one must have of the notion of the Universal Base (*kun gzhi*), explained in the *Lamp Clarifying the Oral Advice on the Universal Base* (*Kun gzhi zhal shes gsal ba'i sgron ma*).[56]

These various works help provide a better understanding of the contents of the *Six Lamps* and the precise instructions revealed by Tapihritsa. They are of course of great help for the translator since clarifications are made possible by consulting these texts. In the course of preparing this translation I have used the following six versions of the *Zhangzhung Nyengyü* containing the root-text:

- the xylographic version prepared by Yongdzin Sangye Tenzin in Tibet and published in *History and Doctrines of Bon po Nispanna Yoga*,

---

55. English translations of all four works have been prepared and will eventually be published by Editions Khyung-Lung.

56. This work was translated into French, together with two commentaries (abridged and enlarged), in Achard, *La Lampe Clarifiant les Conseils sur la Base Universelle*, Editions Khyung-Lung, 2009.

- photocopies and photos of the Samling (bSam gling) manuscript,

- the Nyarong xylographic edition prepared by Shardza Rinpoche (1859–1934) and Welter Sang-ngak Lingpa (1864–1959?),

- the manuscript included in the Welkhyung Gompa Kanjur, as preserved by Kundröl Möngyel Lhasé Rinpoche in the reprint of the Kanjur,

- the manuscript reprinted in the second edition of the Kanjur in Chengdu (ca. 1990) known as the *Ayong Kanjur*, and

- the recent edition included in volume 24 of the Gangs ti se bon gzhung collection, which essentially reprints the Nyarong xylographic print.

PART ONE
INSTRUCTIONS
ON THE SIX LAMPS

Extracted from the Oral Transmission
of the Great Perfection in Zhangzhung

Preface

Homage to Kuntuzangpo, the omniscient Self-Awareness!

While the great Gyerpung Nangzher Löpo was residing
West of Drajé, in the solitude of his rock cave of Drak
    Shawadong,
The Emanation Body of the Lord Tapihritsa came (to him)
And, having subdued (Gyerpung's) arrogant pride,
Revealed to him the abiding mode of Awareness.

Being set free from the chains of all fetters (hindering him),
(Gyerpung) was propelled on the plain of Equality (of the
    Base)
And was made to take hold of the natural state of Awareness.

Then, after five years had elapsed,
While Gyerpung Chenpo was living in solitude on the island
    of the (Darok) Lake,
In the afternoon of the fifteenth day of the first summer month,

Gyerpung was remaining in contemplation,
When he saw in the sky before him
The Emanation Body of the Lord Tapihritsa,
In an immaculate Body, (pure) like the color of white crystal,
In a self-arisen Body devoid of adornments,
Abiding naked in a Body free from obscurations.

Having generated faith and devotion (for the master),
(Gyerpung) circumambulated and prostrated before him,
After which the Lord told him:

O Fortunate Son of Noble Clan!
You who are endowed with the karmic training of previous
    lifetimes,
Listen and be attentive to the revelation of the real meaning!
In order to guide the fortunate ones of future generations on a
    path without error,
I shall reveal to you the three parts[57] of my profound heart advice.

---

57. The text literally says: "three words" (*tshig gsum*). Here Dru Gyelwa Yungdrung
(and incidentally Yongdzin Rinpoche, who follows the same explanation)
describes these three "parts" as referring to the inner, secret, and innermost secret
sections of the *Zhangzhung Nyengyü*. We can see in the later historical literature (for instance, in the biography of Lunggom Tokmé, one of Yangtön Sherab
Gyeltsen's main disciples) that the expression "the three parts of the secret heart
advice" (*gsang ba'i snying gtam tshig gsum*—the same as the *zab mo'i snying gtam
tshig gsum* of the present text, with the exception of the adjective *profound* instead
of *secret*) definitely refers to the inner, secret, and innermost secret sections of the
Zhangzhung Nyengyü. One should note that in this context Uri Sögyel does not
make any reference to the last three sections of the collection but rather considers the reference as being general, and he reads it as pointing to the transmission
of the oral instructions on the naked seeing of Awareness (*rig pa gcer mthong gi
gdams ngag*, *Ornament of Solar Lights*, p. 359). This may also imply that he considered the *Six Lamps* to belong to the third (and not to the second) section of
the cycle (as can be also seen on p. 356 of his commentary).

If he[58] does not know the ultimate teaching of the 84,000
     doors of Bön,
The innermost quintessence of the teachings of the Great
     Perfection,
The Precepts of the Nine Blissful Ones of the Contemplative
     Transmission,
The Oral Transmission of the Twenty-Four Masters,
The so-called "Six Essential Points of the Pure and Perfect
     Mind,"
Then, the master who reveals these precepts
Will be like (someone) displaying objects to a blind person.
(Therefore), if he lacks these Precepts,
Even if he explains numerous Tantras and Agamas (pertaining
     to) the Great Perfection, (his explanations will be)
Like a body without heart or like sockets without eyes.

Whatever may be his explanations of the 84,000 doors of Bön,
They will exhaust themselves in the vague formulation of the
     conventional meaning
And none of them will enable one to directly reach to the heart
     (of the principle).[59]

It is for this reason, O Son of Noble Clan, that these instructions
Are called "the Mirror in which one identifies the Universal
     Base,"

---

58. As can be seen below, the subject of this line is "the master who reveals these
    precepts."

59. As is evident from the context, this principle is that of Dzogchen itself. Instead of
    snying ("heart"), Dru Gyelwa's *Commentary* reads *gnyen* ("antidote"), which does
    not fit with the context. The Nyarong edition reads *snying*.

"The Lamp that brings forth the hidden secret of Wisdom,"
"The Precept laying Awareness bare in its nakedness,"
"The instruction that pierces and cuts through delusion,"
"The heart advice that directly points out the natural state."

They shall be revealed in:

The Lamp of the Abiding Base, being the key point for identi-
    fying the Universal Base and the way its Essence abides;

The Lamp of the Flesh-Heart, being the key point of the inner
    arising of Self-Awareness and of the Base on which it abides;

The Lamp of the White and Smooth Channel, being the key
    point of Transparent Wisdom and of the path through
    which it shoots up;

The Water Lamp of the Far-Reaching Lasso, being the key
    point of the naked vision of Awareness and of the door to
    which it arises;

The Lamp of Direct Introductions to the Pure Realms, being
    the key point of the decisive certainty regarding the Three
    Bodies and the manner to practice the Path; and

The Lamp of the Moment of the Bardo, being the key point
    of the manner in which saṃsāra and nirvāṇa separate
    and of the frontier that is reached between delusion and
    realization.

O Son of Noble Clan! Don't even utter a single word of these
    instructions
To egoist people without faith and corrupted with wrong
    views,
To distracted people who are uncertain and despise humbleness,
Nor to vulgar and childish people of inferior Vehicles.

Reveal them to people who aspire to Perfect Purity and deeply
   fear births and deaths,
To those who have faith, are weariless, and "carry" the master
   on their head,[60]
To those who have renounced mundane activities and practice
   the profound meaning (of the teachings),
To those who are perfect chalices for such instructions!

Having spoken this way, (Tapihritsa) instructed him in the pre-
   cepts of the six kinds of Lamps,
In the six essential points of the Pure and Perfect Mind.
May they not decline until the end of time and may they bring
   benefits to sentient beings!

Samaya!

---

60. To "carry the lama on one's head" or to "place him at the top" (*bla ma gtsug tu
   khur*) simply means to have a sincere devotion for the master who so kindly
   reveals these instructions.

I. The Lamp of the Abiding Base

Homage to Kuntuzangpo, the primordial Buddha (endowed
   with) Self-Awareness!

O Son of Noble Clan!
"The Lamp of the Abiding Base"
Explains the natural state of the Essence of the Base
And the manner in which saṃsāra and nirvāṇa separate.

1. THE NATURAL STATE OF THE BASE

As to the explanation of the natural state of the Base,
Know that it is expressed according to three (themes, namely,)
The Universal Base, Awareness, and the intellect.

1-1. The Universal Base
As for the Universal Base, the Pure and Perfect Mind,
It is the empty Clear-Light, uncorrected and unaltered.

Its Great Primordial Purity or Absolute Body
Is totally immaculate and unaffected by limitations.

Its Spontaneous Nature or Body of Perfection
Is entirely perfect, fully perfect, totally perfect.

Its undetermined and neutral Emanation Body
Arises in all kinds of impartial marvels.

(Yet this Base) is not divided into individual (partialities):
Just like the sky entirely (embraces) manifested existence,
It encompasses the whole of saṃsāra-nirvāṇa.

Its unique celestial Clarity embraces everything
In a clear sky free from partialities.

Everything arises from its unique, great Expanse,
An empty Expanse that has no dimension.

Everything abides in its unique and great Space,
An equal Space that is neither high nor low.

Thus it is called the "Pure and Perfect Mind,"
Which is explained as being threefold according to the conven-
    tional meaning,[61]

---

61. Yongdzin Rinpoche defines this threefold mode as that of the Universal Base
    (*kun gzhi*), Awareness (*rig pa*), and the mind (*blo* or *sems*). Dru Gyelwa and Uri
    Sögyel define that mode as that of the Sky (*mkha'*), Reality (*bon nyid*), and Mind
    (*sems nyid*). Yongdzin Rinpoche places his interpretation in the perspective of the
    structure of the first part of this chapter (indeed, dealing with the Universal Base,
    Awareness, and the mind as forming in reality the Single Thiglé). Dru Gyelwa

While it is undifferentiated according to the real meaning,
Abiding as the Single Great Thiglé.

Samaya!

1-2. Awareness
The "Wisdom of Awareness"
Is the Awareness arising from within the expanse of the
    Universal Base
In the same way the sun (shines) in the expanse of the sky.

Luminous in its Essence while empty in its Nature,
This knowing Awareness is free from concepts.

In it[62] arises the threefold dynamism of visions,
Namely that of sounds, lights, and rays:
It[63] arises as lights in the clear sky,
(Reverberates as) self-arisen sounds from within the empty
    Expanse,
And projects itself as the rays of nondual Awareness.

---

and Uri Sögyel follow the traditional interpretation of the actual meaning associated with the example (*dpe*, i.e., the sky), the principle (*don*, i.e., Reality), and the sign (*rtags*, i.e., Mind itself). It is however clear that both explanations amount to the same meaning. On the three modalities of example, principle, and sign, see P. Kvaerne, *The Stages of A-khrid Meditation*, pp. xvii–xviii, 44–45. See also Achard, *The Instructions on the Primordial A*, p. 35.

62. Or "from it" (*de las*) if one is to follow Dru Gyelwa's reading of the root-text. The reading "in it" (*de la*) is retained by Uri.

63. The subject of the entire passage is, as expected, the threefold dynamism of Awareness itself.

This (dynamism) is known as that of the "manifested objects."
(Yet,) these objects and Awareness are not separated,
Since they are linked as an inseparable pair,
Which is called the Wisdom of Awareness,
The Universal Base of the continuity of wakeful Awareness,
The Base of the Qualities of the Mirror-Like Wisdom,
The Consciousness of the Universal Base or Base of propensities.

In its total and unmixed perfection,
The (Wisdom) of Awareness arises in the mental continuum of
    each (being).[64]
The Universal Base[65] is neutral and free from conceptions,
And even though its Essence is primordially pure and
    immaculate,
It still abides as the Base of both saṃsāra and nirvāṇa, defects
    and qualities.

64. This verse uses the rare expression *rig pa'i sems* ("the mind of Awareness"). All ver-
    sions of the text that I have used have indeed *rig pa'i sems* (Uri Sögyel's *Commen-
    tary* also has the same reading), although Dru Gyelwa's *Commentary* explicitly
    reads this verse as "the Wisdom of Awareness arises in each mental continuum"
    (*rig pa'i ye shes sems rgyud so sor shar*), which is by far more explicit. The expres-
    sion *rig pa'i sems* or *rig pa'i sems rgyud* also occurs in the *Lamp Clarifying the
    Oral Advice on the Universal Base*, as well as in the *Twenty-One Seals*. It is not
    that diffused or frequently used in general Dzogchen literature. I have chosen
    Dru Gyelwa's rendering in the translation since the literal meaning of *rig pa'i sems
    rgyud so sor shar* might induce a wrong understanding of the principle that is
    being described.

65. As shown by Uri's *Commentary*, the Universal Base (*kun gzhi*) and the Wisdom
    of Awareness (*rig pa'i ye shes*) are one, i.e., they are two interchangeable expres-
    sions in this context.

(Thus,) through the link between lights and Awareness,

It becomes the Base of (Buddha) Bodies and (ordinary) bodies.

Through the link between sounds and Awareness,

It becomes the Base of the Speech (of the Buddhas) and (ordinary) speech.

And through the link between rays and Awareness,

It becomes the Basis of the (Buddha) Mind and the (ordinary) mind.

Samaya!

1-3. The intellect

As to the "ordinary thinking mind,"[66]

Even though the King of wakeful Awareness is free from conceptions,

It is still the Base in which arises the diversity of thoughts and recollections:

(Therefore,) just like luminous rays (emanating) from the dynamism of the sun,

The intellect arises from the dynamism of Awareness.

The various thoughts and recollections are then involved with objects

And the six associations[67] arise as the dynamism (apprehending) the six objects (of the senses).

---

66. Literally "mind of the intellect" (*blo'i sems*).

67. Of consciousnesses.

This is called the "thinking intellect."
It is named "recollection" because it remembers and under-
    stands (things)
And "mind" since it is involved with objects.

Samaya!

1-4. The summary
If we sum this up, it is as follows:
What we call Universal Base, Awareness, and intellect,
Base, essence, and marvels,
Mother, Son, and Dynamism,
As well as mind and Mind itself,
Abide in the following manner, without union or disunion
In the continuum of an individual:

The Universal Base is like the extent of the sky,
Awareness is like the quintessence of the sun,
The intellect is like the luminous rays of the sun,
Sounds appear in a self-arisen dynamism,
Lights are like domes of rainbows and solar lights, and
Rays (spread in) the mode of networks of solar rays.
Such is the natural state of the primordial condition.

Samaya!

2. THE SEPARATION BETWEEN SAMSĀRA AND NIRVĀNA

As for the manner in which saṃsāra and nirvāṇa separated,
How did Kuntuzangpo primordially awaken himself?
And how did sentient beings (start to) wander in saṃsāra
    because of their karma?
It is because of his realization that Kuntuzangpo primordially
    awakened himself,
And it is owing to their nonrealization that sentient beings err
    in saṃsāra because of their karma.
The Universal Base and Awareness are the basis for realization
    and delusion;
The three manifested objects are the circumstances (leading to)
    realization and delusion;
The consciousness that knows and recollects is the cause for
    realization and delusion.

(However,) the Universal Base and Awareness are (in reality)
    free from realization and delusion;
They do not part in dichotomies (such as) saṃsāra and nirvāṇa;
It is therefore to the intellect that recollects
That realization and delusion occur
And that saṃsāra and nirvāṇa arise as two (distinct modes).

As for the reason (explaining) how realization occurs,
When the dynamism of the three manifested objects arises,[68]
The mind consciousness that thinks and recollects
Sees them clearly as illusory self-manifestations.

---

68. These three manifested objects (*snang ba'i yul gsum*) are sounds, lights, and rays.

Because of these self-manifested objects,
Awareness appears in all its bare nakedness and
The Universal Base is clearly realized as being untainted.

Owing to this realization, Awareness remains in its natural
    state;
It no longer follows after the traces of manifested objects
And, at that time, concretely manifests its own power over
    itself.

The emanations of Nirvāṇa (then appearing)
Arise naturally without (having to be) accomplished.
By virtue of the links between lights and Awareness,
All the emanations of the Body arise;
By virtue of the links between sounds and Awareness,
All the emanations of Speech arise; and
By virtue of the links between rays and Awareness,
All the emanations of the Mind arise.

From this threefold dynamism of Body, Speech, and Mind,
Qualities and Activities arise spontaneously;
(However,) this is not (the result of) collecting the two
    accumulations,[69]
Since it in fact arises spontaneously due to the power of
    realization.

Samaya!

69. Accumulation of merit and wisdom.

As to the reasons (explaining) how sentient beings have
    become deluded,
When the three manifested objects concretely appeared,
Their mind consciousness that thinks and recollects became
    mistaken about (these) objects:
Ignoring these self-manifestations to be illusory, (beings) saw
    them really as manifestations coming from somewhere else
    (than themselves)
And thus covered the principle of Awareness with a mind see-
    ing (things as being something) else (than they are).

Not recognizing their Self-Awareness, they did not realize the
    principle of the Universal Base
And this formed the simultaneously born ignorance.

Because of this ignorance, their consciousness moved toward
    objects
So that they examined manifested objects and grasped at
    them:
This is what is designated as "the mental consciousness."
Because it moved toward objects, consciousness was not con-
    trolled.
Since consciousness was not controlled, it disturbed the three
    manifested objects.
Since the three manifested objects were disturbed, the five
    causal elements arose.[70]
With the arising of these five causal elements, the manifesta-
    tions of the five objects arose.[71]

70. These are fire, water, earth, wind, and space.

71. These are forms, sounds, smells, tastes, and touch.

With the arising of the manifestations of the five objects, the
consciousnesses of the five doors arose.[72]

Thus the six associations (of consciousnesses)[73] scrutinized
objects and fragmented them into a multiple variety (of
phenomena).

Such is the conceptual ignorance.

Because of this conceptual ignorance, they grasped at self and
others,

And because of this grasping at self and others, the five poisons
of the passions arose.[74]

This constitutes the consciousness of afflicted mind.

By the power of the five poisons, conditioned activities arose,

And because of these activities and passions, karmic propensities were collected on the Base.

(Thus,) the nonconceptual Universal Base[75] (becomes) the
Base where karmic propensities are collected,[76]

---

72. These are eyes, ears, nose, tongue, and body consciousness.

73. This refers to the consciousnesses of the five senses to which is added the mental
consciousness.

74. These are desire and attachment, wrath and aversion, pride, jealousy, and
delusion.

75. Yongdzin Rinpoche explains here that the Universal Base is nonconceptual (*rtog
med*), just like the consciousnesses of the five senses. It does not function with or
depend on concepts at all. Because of this neutrality and because of ignorance, it
becomes the "place" where karmic traces are stored.

76. This whole process is described at length in Achard, *La Lampe Clarifiant les Conseils sur la Base Universelle*, which contains a translation and two commentaries on
the *Kun gzhi zhal shes gsal ba'i sgron ma*, an appendix to the *Six Lamps*. Samten
Karmay (*The Great Perfection*, p. 183) was the first to note that this essential idea
of *kun gzhi* becoming the ground where karmic traces are stored is the perfect

The six collections of consciousnesses are the agents collecting
    karmic propensities,
While karma and passions (cause) the accumulation of mul-
    tiple karmic propensities
Grasped by the defiled mind, which does not let them go away.

As the power of these karmic propensities intensified,
Mental bodies made of discursive thoughts were concretely
    produced
And strayed into the Formless Realm because of delusion.[77]

When the power of these karmic propensities intensified and
    became coarser than before,
Bodies of lights made of visionary appearances were concretely
    produced
And strayed cyclically into the Form Realm because of anger.

When the power of these karmic propensities intensified
    (even) more than that,

---

answer to questions asking how the primordially pure Base of the natural state can
become the base of delusion.

77. *gTi mug* is rendered here as delusion, which is a form of very gross stupidity
or absence of understanding. Some translators render it as ignorance, but thus
the difference between *gti mug* (*moha*) and *ma rig pa* (*āvidya*) is lost. Ignorance (*āvidya*) is the incapacity to recognize the dynamism of the natural state
and apprehending it as a manifestation having another source than oneself
(*gzhan snang*). Delusion (*moha*) is a form of wandering due to attachment to
conditioned existence. Cosmologically, ignorance comes first, and then delusion appears, together with desire and hatred (or, in the case of the five poisons,
together with desire, hatred, jealousy, and pride).

Material bodies made of flesh and blood were concretely
   produced
And strayed into the Desire Realm because of desire-
   attachment.
Then, because of the connection between the three (manifestations)—sounds, lights, and rays—and Awareness,
Body, speech, and mind—these three (doors)—were concretely
   produced.

Because of the karmic propensities accumulated by the six
   associations (of consciousnesses), they[78] strayed into the
   manifestations of the six destinies.

Because of the five poisons of the passions, they strayed into
   the five saṃsāric paths.[79]

From the four elements (acting as) causes and conditions,[80]
   four kinds of births were produced.[81]

From flesh, blood, heat, and breath arose the (illnesses of the)
   four kinds of constituents.[82]

---

78. The referent here is "the three doors" (*sgo gsum*), in other words, the triple con-
    tinuum of the individual.

79. These correspond to the destinies of (1) denizens of hells, (2) hungry ghosts, (3)
    animals, (4) human beings, and (5) both demigods and gods.

80. "Acting as great causes" (*rgyu chen*) according to the reading of the Nyarong ver-
    sion (p. 206). In this case, these "great causes" are the four elements themselves
    (earth, water, fire, and air).

81. Births from eggs, miracles, wombs, and heat (or moisture).

82. This refers to illnesses associated with wind, bile, phlegm, and their combination.

Because Awareness is connected to lights, the Vessels, and Elix-
    irs, bodies and minds emerged.

As to the way in which the worlds of the outer Vessels arose
    from[83] the mind,
Owing to the connection between the light of the sky and
    Awareness,
A flickering wind appeared, moving here and there;
From the power of its movements, a hot fire appeared;
From the fights between fire and wind, hot and cold, humidity
    appeared as water.
From the elixir of water, the earth that was generated served as
    a basis.

All the worlds of the (outer) Vessels were produced from
    this,
With the emergence of the manifestations of the five objects[84]
    from the elixir of the elements (acting as their) five causes.
Such is the way in which the worlds of the outer Vessels
    emerged from[85] the mind.

As to the way in which sentient beings forming the Inner Elix-
    irs arose from[86] the mind,

83. One should correct *la* ("to") to *las* ("from").

84. Forms, sounds, smells, taste, and touch.

85. Again correcting *la* to *las*.

86. Most versions of the text have *sems la shar* ("arose to the mind"), which does not
    make much sense. The correct reading is given at the end of this section, with the
    text saying *sems las shar* ("arose from the mind"). See Nyarong ed., p. 206.

Because of the connection between the light of the sky and
Awareness,
The thinking mind and the moving winds appeared.

Because the winds and mind are connected, the swirling breath
appeared.
From the power of breath arose heat, the element of fire.

Because of the aggregation of breath and heat arose blood, the
element of water.
From the elixir of blood arose flesh, the element of earth.

Because the body and mind are connected, the five essential
organs were created
And established as the supports of the five kinds of elements.

From the five limbs also emerged the dynamism of the five elements (while)
The elixir of the five elements was collected into the five inner
cavities.
The doors of the five elements also opened in the five sense
organs (while)
The five dynamisms of the five consciounesses developed
individually,
Grasping and enjoying individually the five objects.
Such is (the way) sentient beings—the inner Elixirs—arose
from the mind.

Because the five elements are connected to the mind, the five
poisons of the passions were generated:

Because the sky is connected to the mind, anger was generated;

Because the breath is connected to the mind, pride was
generated;

Because heat is connected to the mind, jealousy was generated;

Because blood is connected to the mind, desire was generated;

Because flesh is connected to the mind, stupidity[87] was
generated.

Because the five poisons are connected to the five elements, the
five kinds of aggregates were generated:

Because anger is connected to the sky, the aggregate of consciousness was generated;

Because pride is connected to the breath, the aggregate of
formations was generated;

Because jealousy is connected to heat, the aggregate of cogni-
tions was generated;

Because desire is connected to blood, the aggregate of sensa-
tions was generated;

Because stupidity is connected to flesh, the aggregate of form
was generated.

Because of the connection between the five aggregates and the
five poisons,

Various conditioned actions[88] and conducts appeared.

87. As we have seen, generally, most English translators do not differentiate between
ma rig pa (ignorance) and *gti mug* (stupidity, delusion, etc.). Both have, however,
specific semantic fields and are not the same. See above in note 77.

88. *'du byed (kyi) las*, formational or volitional actions that concretely correspond to
the second of the twelve links (on which see note 91 below).

From the cause and condition linking[89] actions and passions,
The general and specific sufferings of saṃsāra appeared.

Since times without beginnings and in endless saṃsāra,
We have taken up bodies in the five (destinies of) migration,
    cyclically (roaming in) the three Realms:[90]
The twelve links of dependent origination[91] turned the wheel
    of existence,
Not propelled by evil actions but appearing through the power
    of ignorance.
Thus, even though saṃsāra and nirvāṇa emerge as two (sepa-
    rate modes),

89. Correcting *'brel bas* to *'brel ba'i* according to the Nyarong version (fol. 6b).

90. The three Realms (*khams gsum*) are the Realm of Desire (*'dod khams*), the Realm of Form (*gzugs khams*), and the Formless Realm (*gzugs med kyi khams*). The five destinies of migration are (1) those of the denizens of hells, (2) those of hungry ghosts, (3) those of animals, (4) those of human beings, and (5) those of both gods and demigods. Some versions of the root-text have the six destinies of migration in which, as we have seen, the destinies of demigods and gods are distinguished. Otherwise, the meaning is actually the same.

91. The links are (1) ignorance, (2) formation, (3) consciousness, (4) name and form;,(5) the six sense sources, (6) contact, (7) sensation, (8) craving, (9) grasping, (10) becoming, (11) birth, and (12) old age and death. The Base of the natural state of the Mind is spontaneously endowed with a dynamism (*rtsal*) manifesting in what is designated as the manifestations of the Base (*gzhi snang*). When these manifestations are not recognized for what they are, there is *ignorance*. Because of ignorance, there is *formation* of karma. This karma causes the manifestations of the *consciousness* in the next rebirth. Through this rebirth, one's consciousness acquires *name and form*. This form is endowed with sense faculties, which are the *six sense sources*. Through the functions of these senses, one enters into *contact* with objects, which generates *craving* and subsequently *grasping*. Because of this grasping, one produces the causes of *becoming* that leads to a new existence. Through this becoming, one endures *rebirth* in a particular destiny in which one eventually suffers from *old age and death*.

They are (actually) manifestations perceived by minds that are
   either realized or not realized.
In reality, saṃsāra and nirvāṇa are not dually separated
But abide as the Single Thiglé, the great Equality.

The Lamp of the Abiding Base is hereby completed.

Samaya!

II. The Lamp of the Flesh-Heart

Homage to Kuntuzangpo, the natural Awareness arising from within!

O Son of Noble Clan!
Here is the (explanation of) the Lamp of the Flesh-Heart, the Base on which (Awareness) abides, the so-called "key point of the inner arising of natural Awareness":[92]

92. The teachings associated with each Lamp form a key point (*gnad*) in themselves, dealing with specific themes. Here, the teachings associated with the Lamp of the Flesh-Heart (*tsitta sha'i sgron ma*) actually make up what is known as the "key point of the inner arising of natural Awareness." The Lamp of the Flesh-Heart is thus to be understood as a Base (*gzhi*) from which Awareness naturally arises. As we shall see, the next Lamp will be considered to be a Path (*lam*), or rather a pathway, for the arising of Transparent Wisdom (*ye shes zang thal*). The fourth Lamp will be described as the arising door (*'char sgo*) of this Wisdom, while the fifth will correspond to its visionary marvels. The last one is the key point expounding bardo teachings.

Thus, since realization and delusion appear dually to the think-
    ing mind,
Saṃsāra and nirvāṇa emerge in a dual (mode); however,
The Universal Base and Awareness do not experience delusion
    or realization
Throughout past, present, and future.
They therefore do not experience being separated into saṃsāra
    and nirvāṇa.

Well then, on which Base presently abides
This quintessence, which expresses itself since the beginning
As the Universal Base that has never experienced
    obscurations
And as Awareness that has never experienced delusion?

It dwells in the luminous matrix of space, the radiant sky,
Which is the Brown Cornelian Tent with crystal beams,
The Luminous Tent of Clear Visions.

(This sanctuary) is called *Shethün Tsadzin*, "Holding the
    Channels of the Heart."
Outwardly, it abides as an eight-cornered jewel, while inwardly
    it abides as an eight-petaled lotus
In the center of which the five lights abide like a pitched rain-
    bow tent.

In that (vast) expanse, the Universal Base and Awareness
Are not mixed with anything but abide immaculate as the
    Great Primordial Purity.

However, even though the Universal Base entirely embraces
     the body, like the sky,
It is obscured by the clouds of delusion and does not radiate,
(While at the same time), like a cloudless sky, in the center of
     the heart,
Wisdom abides as the Great Luminous Expanse.

Even though Awareness abides as entirely pervading the body,
     like the sun,
It is obscured by the darkness of discursive thoughts and does
     not radiate,
(While at the same time), like a sun free from darkness, in the
     center of the heart,
Self-Awareness abides as the "Great Inner Arising."

Just like the sun shining in a cloudless sky,
They abide in the center of the heart, in the mode of the undif-
     ferentiated Mother and Son.

(On its side,) the thinking mind, similar to the luminous rays
     of the sun,
Ascends the pathway of the channels, relying on the heart:
It thus enjoys and grasps objects through the doorway of the
     senses.

How then do the illusory body and the mind unite and
     separate?
The Universal Base is like the sky: it embraces everything;
Awareness is like a bird: it abides in its own dimension in the
     sky.

The intellect is like the wings of the bird: it drives it every-
    where.[93]
The body is like a trap: it holds the feathered bird in the trap.
The bird and the trap unite and then separate but
They do not unite with and separate from the space of the sky,[94]
For (the latter) does not rely on anything but abides as all-
    embracing.[95]

(Similarly,) the Universal Base is like the ground: it embraces
    everything;
Awareness is like a man, abiding there in his own place.
The intellect is like a horse, leading him everywhere.
The body is like shackles, so that the man can hold the horse
    prisoner.

93. Some versions of the text have the verb *spyod* instead of *bskyod*. This last reading
    (*bskyod*) appears in the Nyarong version, which is generally more reliable. The
    verb *bskyod* is confirmed by Dru Gyelwa in his *Commentary* (p. 233). Uri's *Com-
    mentary* is less systematic with this part of the root-text, since it does not quote
    the text literally (bypassing the possible confusion with *spyod* and *bskyod*). In
    fact, Dru Gyelwa is not consistent either when commenting on this section of
    the root-text, since he combines the three series of similes that are used here,
    commenting on them collectively instead of basing his discourse on a line-by-
    line approach. However, the verb *bskyod* can still be found in this section of his
    Commentary.

94. This line is missing from the Welkhyung Kanjur version of the text (p. 206). It is
    present in all other versions consulted. Moreover, the last two lines of the three
    similes given in this part of the text appear as a leitmotif, which proves that the
    absence of this line in the Kanjur version is indeed a mistake (implying that the
    existence of this line in other versions is not an interpolation that was added and
    copied in ulterior editions of the text).

95. Following the oral teachings of Yongdzin Rinpoche, these obscure lines simply
    mean that just as the bird and the trap unite and separate within a space which
    is that of the sky, similarly the mind and the body unite and separate within the
    Space of the Universal Base, not elsewhere.

The shackles, the man, and the horse unite and separate, but
They do not unite with and separate from the space of the
    ground,
For (the latter) does not rely on anything but abides as all-
    embracing.

The Universal Base is like the ocean, embracing everything;
Awareness is like a fish, abiding there in its own place;
The intellect is like the fish's fins, enabling it to move every-
    where.
The body is like a net, so that the fish is ensnared in the net.
The net and the fish unite and separate but
They do not unite with or separate from the space of the ocean,
For (the latter) does not rely on anything but abides as all-
    embracing.

Thus he spoke.

The Lamp of the Flesh-Heart is hereby completed.

Samaya!

III. The Lamp of the White and Smooth Channel

Homage to Kuntuzangpo, the Body of Transparent Wisdom!

O Son of Noble Clan!
Here is the Lamp of the White and Smooth Channel, the Path
    through which (Awareness) arises,
The so-called "key point of the Transparent Wisdom":

Because this primordially abiding quintessence, (which consists
    of) the Universal Base and Awareness,
Has a sanctuary located in the center of the heart and
A path emerging in a self-arisen mode in the pathway of the
    channels,
The explanation of the way body and mind arise from[96] the
    Pure and Perfect Mind is as follows:

---

96. Here again one should correct *la* into *las*. This reading is confirmed by the Nya-
    rong xylograph (fol. 8a.5).

When the body and the mind unite in the mother's womb,
The sky makes space for them, while the earth generates and
    supports (their union);
Water unites them as one and also nourishes them;
The heat of fire sublimates the body and the mind (while)
The wind separates purity from impurity and cleanses the cav-
    ity of the channels.

The existence of the outer body is then produced from the
    navel,
While the existence of the inner mind emerges from the
    heart:
The heart (itself) is first produced from the mixture of the
    white and red (Thiglés)
And is the support of the sky element.

Then, in[97] the center of the heart, through the dynamism of
    lights and Awareness,
The wind of the sky element emerges,
Opening the doorway of the channel of the heart.

From there, the upward moving wind opens the cavity of the
    central channel further up,
Passing through the center of the Wheel of Enjoyment in the
    throat.
It pierces through the Wheel of Great Bliss, on the top of the
    head

97. Some versions (such as the Gangs ti se bon gzhung, p. 209) have "from" (nas), but
here I follow the reading given in the Nyarong xylograph (fol. 8b.1).

And its (upper) door comes forth in the pure aperture[98] on the
   crown of the head:
This is the Pathway of Nirvāṇa.

The downward eliminating wind opens the cavity of the central
   channel further down,
Passing through the center of the Wheel of Emanations in the
   navel.
It pierces through the ladder of the sacrum (connecting) the
   joints (of the vertebrae)
And its (lower) door comes forth in the Wheel of Methods
   and Knowledge, in the secret place:
This is the Pathway of Saṃsāra.
From the ladder of the sacrum (connecting) the joints (of the
   vertebrae)
The two channels of saṃsāra and nirvāṇa branch out from the
   central channel:
Supported on the right and left,
They pass through the opening of the occiput,
Journey through the membrane of the brain,
And draw in downward at the level of[99] the two eyebrows,
(Eventually) opening in the two nostrils.

98. *spyi gtsug tshangs pa'i bu ga* can also be understood as the Brahma (*tshangs pa*)
   opening on the crown of the head. Generally in the Bön tradition this Brahma
   aperture (*tshangs pa'i bu ga*, skt. *brahmarandra*) is not defined as being associated with Brahma (*tshangs pa*) but is understood literally as being endowed with
   a pure quality (*tshangs pa*, same word). This is the justification for the present
   choice of translation (but in any case, both meanings refer to the same opening,
   even though the second interpretation favors a Hinduist influence that is not
   relevant here).

99. Literally "from between the juncture of the two eyebrows" (*smin mtshams gnyis
   nas*).

The right one is the channel of saṃsāra, (in which)
Flow the impure Thiglés of the physical constituents
And the wind of passions, (causing) the arising of a multitude
    of defects.

The left one is the channel of nirvāṇa, (in which)
Flow the pure Thiglés of the mind and the wind of Wisdom,
(Causing) the arising of a multitude of qualities.

No defect or quality whatsoever moves through the central
    channel,
(Thus letting) Awareness arise in its Great Primordial
    Purity.

These three channels constitute the channels of the sky of the
    Universal Base.
The heart abides like a pitched tent while
The three channels abide in the mode of its main poles.[100]
Then, in the center of the heart,
Through the dynamism of lights and Awareness,
Arise the four winds of the elements
Opening the cavities of channels,
Like pulling the ropes of a tent in the four directions:
The four vital organs being then formed,
They are established as the supports of the four elements.

---

100. *Srog shing*, literally "life-tree," referring to the beams or poles used when pitching
    a tent.

Then, from the five vital organs,
Arise the five winds of the branch elements,
Which open the cavities of channels so that the five branch
elements come out.

From there, the winds of the secondary elements separate into
(two) fivefold sets:
In the head they branch into the five sense organs,
While in the four limbs, they divide into the fivefold sets of
fingers (and toes).

Then, from the five vital organs,
The five winds of the pure elements arise:
Opening the cavities of channels upward,
They let the doorways of the five elements come forth as the
doorways of the five sense supports
So that the doorways of the five elements can shine over their
five objects.

Inside the cavity of these five channels
(Glows) the radiance of the five lights
From which the pure essence of the five elements arise in the
respective (sense organs);
This generates the dynamism through which the five conscious-
nesses investigate the five objects,
And this is what one calls "the five sense organs."

Then, from the five vital organs
Arise the five winds of the impure elements:

Opening the cavities of channels downward,
They produce the five kinds of entrails, which are the vessels of
    the elements.
Inside of these move[101] the five samaya substances, which are
    the elixir of the five elements.

Thus, the three channels constitute the trunk.
Those channels of the elements form its branches,
Which divide into 360 limbs,
Separating into 21,000 secondary limbs.

With those dividing into 84,000 leaves,
The dynamism of consciousness appears multifarious.

Thus, even though channels arise in manifold ways,
(What one calls) "Lamp of the Channel" is the central
    channel,
And even though the Universal Base
Entirely embraces the channels, like the sky,
It is obscured by the clouds of delusion and does not radiate.
(However,) in the pathway of the central channel, its Wisdom
    shines forth
In a total transparency, like in a cloudless sky.

Even though Awareness abides as entirely pervading
The channels, like the sun (shining in the sky),

101. *rgyu* is the verb that has been retained for the translation. The Nyarong edition
    gives the reading *chags*. If this latter reading is the correct one, then the line must
    be corrected to: "Inside of these are produced the five samaya substances, which
    are the elixir of the five elements."

It is obscured by the darkness of discursive thoughts and does
   not radiate.
(However,) in the pathway of the central channel, which is like
   a sun free from darkness,
Self-Awareness arises in its Great Primordial Purity.

Like the sun shining in a cloudless sky,
The Mother and the Son emerge in the central pathway in an
   inseparable mode.

Thus he spoke.

*The Lamp of the White and Smooth Channel is hereby
   completed.*

Samaya!

IV. The Water Lamp of the Far-Reaching Lasso

Homage to Kuntuzangpo, the Body of naturally arising Wisdom!

O Son of Noble Clan!
Here is the Water Lamp of the Far-Reaching Lasso, the doorway to which (Awareness) arises,
The so-called "key point through which one sees Awareness in
its nakedness":

Thus, this quintessence, which abides since the beginning (as)
the Universal Base and Awareness,
Has a ground located in the center of the heart
And a Path that, having ascended the way of the channels,
Arises to its door, the Water Lamp;

In the middle of the brain, in the Conch Mansion,

Is a channel known as Tsangri Purlang[102] (branching) from the
central (channel).

Its single root divides into two extremities, which open within
the eyes:[103]

The doors of this channel appear like blossoming sesame flowers

And are the doorways through which the visions of Awareness
come forth.

From the cavity of this channel,

The five lights shine like peacock feathers.

To the door where these lights are contemplated,

The sky-like Mother[104]—the Universal Base—

Shines as the all-pervasive Wisdom devoid of outer and inner
(distinctions).

As to Awareness, it arises to its visionary door like the quintessence[105] of the sun, without concept.

As to the intellect, being like the rays of the sun,

(It manifests) in various thought patterns engaged (in grasping
at) objects.

As to the lights, they are the natural lights of Awareness,

Shining in the sky in the manner of rainbow abodes.

102. *Tsang ri* means "channel" in the Zhangzhung language and *Purlang* means
"head." Therefore *Tsangri Purlang* means "the channel of the head."

103. The section "which opens within the eyes" is missing in the Nyarong version
(fol. 10a.2).

104. The term "Mother" (*ma*) is missing in the Nyarong version (ibid.).

105. "Quintessence" is missing in the Nyarong version.

As to rays, they are the natural rays of Awareness,
Shining in visions in the manner of nets of solar rays.

Thus, the quintessence that abides in this way since the
    beginning
Arises clearly and concretely at the doorway of the senses
And, not being produced by the intellect,
(Shines) without fluctuation at the door of the Lamps.
It is consequently known as the "key point of the naked vision
    of Awareness."

[*Thus he spoke.*][106]

The Water Lamp of the Far-Reaching Lasso is hereby completed.

Samaya!

---

106. This is missing in all editions used. The omission is certainly due to the fact that
    the previous line ends up with *ces bya'o*, which is rendered by quotation marks
    " "—and adding any *ces so* or *ces gsungs so* might have appeared redundant.

V. The Lamp of the Direct Introductions to the Pure Realms

Homage to Kuntuzangpo, Self-Awareness arising concretely!

O Son of Noble Clan!
Here is the Lamp of the Direct Introductions to the Pure
    Realms,
(Explaining) how to practice the Path
(and forming) the so-called "key point of gaining decisive
    certainty regarding the Three Bodies"; (it is divided
    into)
The direct introduction to the Three Bodies and
    Gaining decisive certainty.

1. THE DIRECT INTRODUCTION TO THE THREE BODIES

Here is what the direct introduction consists of:

O Son of Noble Clan,

The natural state,[107] the Universal Base that is this Pure and
Perfect Mind itself,

This great all-encompassing display without partiality,

Is the Space of Reality,

And the fact that, in this sanctuary, one's Awareness abides as
the Great Primordial Purity

(Means that) the Absolute Body arises naturally within oneself
and consequently

That the pure realm of the Absolute Body abides within
oneself.

However, even though (this Body) accompanies us continuously (throughout) the three times,

It is said to (abide as) not being recognized.

O Son of Noble Clan!

This Sanctuary, the Brown Cornelian Tent with crystal beams,

This brilliant Citadel of light,

---

107. The term "natural state" (*gnas lugs*) is missing in the Nyarong version (fol.
10b.2). Then, if this reading is the correct one, the whole passage should be
rendered as: "The Universal Base, the Mind of Perfect Purity itself,/ This great
all-encompassing display without partiality/ Is the Space of Reality/," etc. However, in his *Commentary*, Dru Gyelwa reads the line with "natural state" (*gnas
lugs*), while Uri Sögyel reads it with "sanctuary" (*gnas*) only. In his quote of this
passage of the text in his *Treasury of Space and Awareness* (II, p. 356), Shardza
Rinpoche gives the following simpler reading: "O Son of Noble Clan! The Base,
(this) great all-encompassing display" (*rigs kyi bu gzhi khyab bdal chen po phyogs
ris med pa ni/. . .*).

Is the Pure Realm of Ogmin,[108] which cannot be transcended;
The fact that in this Sanctuary, the Wisdom of our
Awareness
Is spontaneously accomplished as sounds, rays, and lights,
And that the whole of saṃsāra and nirvāṇa is spontaneously
    perfected there,
(Means that) the Body of Perfection arises within oneself and
    consequently
That the pure realms of the Perfection Body abide within
    oneself.
But when they are not realized (as such), they arise as deluded
    realms.

O, Son of Noble Clan!
The sanctuary that is complete with its three channels, six
    kinds of Wheels,
Trunk, branches, limbs, and secondary limbs
Is the pure realm of the perfect Wheel of Letters;
In that sanctuary, the Wisdom of one's[109] Awareness (is
    endowed with a)
Dynamism that emerges in the six objects of the six
    consciousnesses;
The fact that it performs the manifold activities of body,
    speech, and mind

---

108. Akaniṣṭha, the highest Buddhafield of the Form Realm, a sanctuary that is never
    destroyed at the end of kalpas.

109. "One's" (*rang*) is missing in the Nyarong version (fol. 11a.1).

(Means that) the Emanation Body emerges within oneself and
    consequently
That the pure realms of the Emanation Body abide within oneself.
But if they are not realized (as such), they arise as the manifes-
    tations of the six destinies.

2. GAINING DECISIVE CERTAINTY

As to the decisive certainty regarding the Three Bodies
During the direct introduction to the Awareness of the Essence
    itself,[110]
One gains decisive certainty regarding the Absolute Body.

During the direct introduction to the Awareness of Superior
    Insight,
One gains decisive certainty regarding the Form Bodies.

The Awareness of the Essence itself is introduced with three
    Lamps:
With the Lamp of the Abiding Base, the Base is identified;
With the Lamp of Illustrative Examples, its allegorical prin-
    ciples are illustrated;
With the Lamp of the Signs of Wisdom, the signs are directly
    introduced.[111]

---

110. Awareness of the Essence itself (*ngo bo nyid kyi rig pa*) simply means our own
    intrinsic Awareness. In this state, one directly and clearly discerns (*rig*) the pri-
    mordially pure Essence (*ngo bo*) of our own primordial condition, not as an
    object but as the self-reflexive knowledge of this state itself.

111. The detail regarding the practice of these three Lamps is given in the following
    paragraphs, starting with the identification of the Base, the direct introduction
    to examples, and the direct introduction to signs.

O Son of Noble Clan!
For identifying the Base,[112]
Leave the Lamps in their own place
And when consciousness is left in its own place,
Without examining objects,
This consciousness does not analyze[113] objects anymore
And abides as being unpolluted by objects.[114]

At that time, within the empty and luminous Universal
    Base,
Clearly radiating without being covered by obscurations,
The manifestations of objects are that which abides clearly
Like reflections emerging on a mirror.

At that time, Awareness
Abides as being limpid without thoughts
And open without fixations,
Maintained without grasping and
Abiding naked without concepts,
While the manifestations of objects are that which arises
    vividly
Like reflections appearing in a crystal sphere.

---

112. As we have seen in the first Lamp, notions related to the Base cover the specific
    representations associated with the Universal Base (*kun gzhi*), Awareness (*rig
    pa*), and the mind or intellect (*blo*).

113. Most versions have *dpyad* (analyze) but some have *spyad* (engage).

114. Correcting *yul gyi shes pa* to *yul gyis shes pa*.

As to the intellect, it corresponds to those manifold memories
and thoughts that distinguish and differentiate objects
individually.

O Son of Noble Clan!
As to the illustration of these principles with examples,
A butter lamp illustrates the natural clarity of Wisdom;
A lotus illustrates its immaculate Primordial Purity;
The heart of the sun illustrates its spontaneous Clear-Light;
A mirror illustrates its natural clarity without obscuration;
A crystal sphere illustrates its transparent nakedness; and
The sky illustrates its omnipervasive Wisdom.

O Son of Noble Clan!
As to the direct introduction to signs,
There are the direct introductions to the principle of the Uni-
versal Base and to that of Awareness.

Regarding the direct introduction to the principle of the Universal Base,
(One first uses) a butter lamp that radiates purely in its own
natural clarity,
Being free from the thick obscurity of darkness.[115]

---

115. The Nyarong version (fol. 11b.4) adds here: "The Universal Base, being free from
the thick darkness of ignorance/ Abides purely in its own natural clarity." This
is probably a case of dittography, since these two lines do not show up in the
commentaries.

To the doorway of the Lamps, the Universal Base (appears)
Free from any thick obscuration whatsoever,
And its Wisdom radiates purely in its own natural clarity.

A lotus, even though abiding in the mud,
Is not polluted by the impurity of the mud
But remains nakedly immaculate.
Thus, to the doorway of the Lamps, the Universal Base[116]
Is not polluted by any impurity whatsoever
But remains naked in its Primordial Purity.

Not created by anyone, the sun
Shines forth resplendently since the beginning in its great
    radiating light.
(In the same way), the Universal Base, (which arises)
At the doorway of the Lamps and which nobody has created,
Is spontaneously accomplished since the beginning as the great
    Clear-Light,
Arising resplendently as the great Self-Arisen Wisdom.

On a mirror, which radiates without being covered by
    obscurations,
All reflections arise in a nonobscured way.
(Similarly,) to the doorway of the Lamps, the Universal Base
Radiates as a self-emerging Wisdom not covered by any
    obscurations
And on which all manifestations of outer objects arise in a
    nonobscured way.

116. This line is missing in the Nyarong version (fol. 12a.1).

A crystal sphere, devoid of a cloth likely to cover it and to
    obscure it,
Abides in its bare and naked transparency.
(In the same way,) to the doorway of the Lamps, the Universal Base
Is free from any cloth likely to cover and obscure it
And abides as the bare and naked Transparent Wisdom.

Just as the sky entirely embraces (everything) without outer or
    inner (distinctions),
At the doorway of the Lamps, the Universal Base
Entirely embraces (all) without outer or inner (distinctions), as
    the great Transparent Wisdom.[117]

O Son of Noble Clan!
As to the direct introduction to the principle of Awareness,
Just as the Universal Base abides,
Awareness abides thus (in the very same way).

As for gaining a decisive certainty regarding its principle,
Let Wisdom be naked, without vesting it with the mantle of
    discursive thoughts!
Leave Awareness in its bare (nature), not contaminated by the
    intellect filled with hate and desires!
Leave the mind in its unaltered natural state, not fabricating
    anything!

117. These two lines are read as follows in the Nyarong version (12b.1): "At the door-
    ways of the Lamps, the Universal Base, free from outer and inner (distinctions),/
    Entirely embraces (everything) as the Primordial Wisdom."

Leave thoughts and concepts without grasping at the traces of
    what is without traces!
Leave the mind in its great Equality, in which (discursive)
    movements do not abound!
Prolong that innate state without cutting the stream of
    Awareness!
The outer Vessels and inner Elixirs, saṃsāra and nirvāṇa,
All these are false, sources of errors that flow into the
    mind.
Thus, by gaining decisive certainty about the fact that all with-
    out exception is the Pure and Perfect Mind,
Manifest Buddhahood is reached right now, without one being
    deceived by delusion.

O Son of Noble Clan!
With the direct introduction to the Awareness of Superior
    Insight,
Here is how to gain decisive certainty regarding the Form
    Bodies:
Move the great Ocean upward,
Focus on the expanse of the dark iron mountains,
And in the visionary matrix of luminous appearances,
You will see nets of magical rays
Similar to intricate cobwebs and necklaces.

In the pitch blackness of the darkness endowed with rays,
You will see luminous citadels, bright and clear,
Similar to rainbows shining in the sky.

In the middle of the swirling conch lake
Arises the doorway of the sound of the empty expanse.
From the secret cavities of the sound in the half-moons,
Reverberates the roar of self-arisen sound,
Rumbling in an unceasing flow.

Subjugate the moving mind on sounds,
Hold the thinking mind on lights,
And train the three dynamisms of Awareness over rays.

By training this triple dynamism on rays,
The maṇḍalas of the Three Bodies will arise in oneself.
Empty marvels will appear as visions
To the empty and selfless Mind itself.

The Wisdom of Self-Awareness has no form but
The Form Bodies of Superior Insight are the dynamism of
      Awareness (itself),
Like the drawing of a rainbow in the sky,
Like an unfolded cloth of brocade,
Like reflections appearing in a mirror.

As to the explanation of the methods for training in this
      dynamism,
Catch in the net of light of the dark cell
The golden fish that move.[118]

---

118. The English language does not have a plural form for *fish* but here it should be
      clear that fish is to be understood as plural.

Direct the mirror of Awareness that illuminates all
Onto the depths of the luminous sky.

Focus the spear of the thinking and conceptual mind
Onto the luminous shields of visions.

At that time, you will see the seeds of the Form Bodies
Like constellations glowing in the sky.

As you get familiar and acquainted with this,
Five kinds of particular familiarizations will appear:
First, the visions will increase
And you will see (manifestations) like mercury (drops) scatter-
    ing and collecting.

Then, the visions will spread
And you will see things larger than the sun and the moon in
    the sky:
You will see the wheels of light of Awareness
As well as the domes of light made up of Thiglés.
Then the visions will intensify
And you will see the maṇḍalas of the Perfection Bodies of the
    Five Clans.

Then the visions will become complete
And you will see the maṇḍalas of spontaneous seals,[119]

119. Uri's *Commentary* clearly shows that this refers to a phase when Thiglés appear
    as garlands of pearls in which Bodies appear. This means that Bodies of deities or
    Buddhas appear in each of these Thiglés.

As well as pure realms (filled with) visionary lights
And marvels free from fluctuations.

Then will come the ultimate stage of visions: (at that stage,)
Lights are (seen as) the natural lights of Awareness,
Empty natural lights (appearing) in the mode of rainbows.

Sounds are (heard as) the natural sounds of Awareness,
Empty natural sounds (appearing) in the mode of echoes.

Rays are (experienced as) the natural rays of Awareness,
Empty marvels (appearing) in the mode of reflections.

Bodies are (seen as) the natural form of Awareness,
Empty reflections (appearing) in the mode of water moons.[120]

The erroneous source of manifestations is then exhausted in
    the mind
And Form Bodies are decisively ascertained within the mind.
The source of delusion is eradicated, and it is therefore impos-
    sible (to err again) into delusion.
The Three Bodies are concretely actualized right now:
(This is why) the power of karma, of cause and fruit, is a great
    lie
And this itself[121] is the powerful method of the Buddhas.

This instruction on the ultimate principle
Is the panacea of those endowed with (proper) training, but

120. I.e., reflections of the moon in water.
121. I.e., the Thögel methods explained above.

It will turn into a poison for those who are deluded.
Thus do not reveal it to all, but keep it secret and hidden.

This milk of a white lioness
Should be poured into fortunate chalices.
To the unfortunate ones who are not proper chalices,
Hold it like the jewel in the throat of a makara[122]
And do not let it dissipate for a thousand kalpas!

Thus he spoke.

*The Lamp of the Direct Introductions to the Pure Realms is
hereby completed!*

Samaya!

122. I.e., like a jewel that is beyond the reach of ordinary beings.

VI. The Lamp of the Moment of the Bardo

Homage to Kuntuzangpo, our Self-Awareness and Manifest Buddhahood!

O Son of Noble Clan!

Here is the Lamp of the Moment of the Bardo,
The frontier where delusion and realization meet,
The so-called "key point of the way in which saṃsāra and nirvāṇa separate";
I will reveal you the way the physical aggregates and the mind separate,
The explanation of the way one liberates if one realizes (one's nature),
And the way one becomes deluded if one does not realize it.

The manner in which body and mind separate is twofold:
The way elements are destroyed and how they fuse together.

The explanation of the way the elements are destroyed is as
    follows:
(When) the spleen and the earth element degenerate,
Your body cannot feel contacts anymore.
You cannot raise your left arm
And the defilements of the nine orifices pour out.

(When) the kidneys and the water element degenerate,
Your ears cannot hear sounds any longer.
You cannot raise your left leg
And you cannot hold your urine anymore.

(When) the liver and the fire element degenerate,
Your tongue cannot feel tastes any longer.
You cannot raise your right arm
And blood (*rakta*)[123] drips from your nose.

(When) the lungs and the air element degenerate,
Your nose cannot sense smells anymore.
You cannot raise your right leg
And you cannot even hold your feces back.

(When) the heart and the sky element degenerate,
Your eyes cannot perceive forms anymore.
You cannot raise your head
And your sperm drips in the secret place.[124]

---

123. The text indeed uses the Sanskrit term *rakta* (blood), while the "common"
    Zhangzhung language equivalents are generally *reg, reg kun,* and *reg thun.*

124. Given the locative *gsang bar* or the genitive *gsang ba'i* readings, the meaning of
    this line changes slightly: (1) *"...and your sperm drips out in the secret [place],"* or

The explanation of the way the elements fuse together is as
    follows:
As earth dissolves into water, you lose your physical strength;
As water dissolves into fire, you also lose your physical luster;
As fire dissolves into air, you also lose your physical heat;
As air dissolves into the mind,
You also lose the capacity to hold your breath;
As the mind dissolves into the Universal Base,
The breath stops and the body and the mind separate.

This moment of death is the frontier between bliss and suffering.
Since (at that time), the propelling power of good and bad
    thoughts is great,
One should impart instructions without error, adapting to the
    capacity of the individual.

O Son of Noble Clan!
The manner in which liberation (occurs) if one realizes (one's
    nature, depends on) the superior, medium, and lower
    (capacities of the individuals).

Just like Garuda chicks or lion cubs, individuals of superior
    capacity
Complete right now the three dynamisms and therefore, as
    soon as their body and mind separate,

---

(2) *"...and the sperm of your secret [place] drips out."* The general meaning is however very clear and refers to the fact that at that time the seminal essence cannot
be held back and spontaneously leaks out without control.

The purity and impurity of their elements are differentiated:

Saṃsāra is stirred up from its depths

And delusion is purified in its own place.

In the sky-like Space of their Universal Base, free from
    partialities,

The sun-like Wisdom of Awareness shines in an all-embracing
    way

While the marvels of the Three Bodies, similar to the rays of
    the sun, arise without exhaustion,

Continuously performing the good of migrating beings.

As to (individuals of) medium capacities, at that time,

The outer manifestations of fire, water, earth, and air stop

And the visions of sounds, lights, and rays arise.

Having separated from the material body made of flesh and
    blood,

Awareness remains naked, without support.

The hosts of karma, passions, and erroneous concepts having
    ceased,

The Universal Base remains uncovered by obscurations.

At that time, owing to the direct introductions to the (Aware-
    ness) of the Essence and of Superior Insight and the (subse-
    quent) familiarization with them,

Six foreknowledges and six rememberings having arisen, one
    reaches full Buddhahood.

As to the six foreknowledges,

Since Awareness remains without support, you know past and
    future lives;

Since the Universal Base remains without obscuration, you
    know the causes and fruits of karma;

Since the gods' eye is perfectly purified, you know pure and
    impure realms;
When the visions of sounds, lights, and rays arise,
You know that this is the Bardo of the Clear-Light of Reality.
Since you have been directly introduced to the Essence itself,[125]
You know that the Three Bodies are spontaneously accom-
    plished in your own mind.
Since you have been directly introduced to Superior Insight,[126]
You know that the natural manifestations of the sounds, lights,
    and rays are the visions of the Three Bodies.

As to the six rememberings,
First you remember that you transmigrate from this life;
Then you remember that this is the bardo;
Then you remember that your Awareness abides without
    support;
Then you remember the oral instructions of your master;
Then you remember that sounds, lights, and rays are your own
    manifestations;
And then you remember that your mind is the Buddha.

You see Awareness in its bare nakedness
And you realize clearly the Universal Base without
    obscuration.
Having realized (this), Awareness takes hold of its natural place
And you don't follow after the traces of manifestations.
By not following the traces of manifestations, these manifesta-
    tions liberate as one's illusory self-manifestations,

125. I.e., to Awareness of the Essence itself (*ngo bo nyid kyi rig pa*).
126. I.e., to Awareness of Superior Insight (*lhag mthong gi rig pa*).

And as these manifestations liberate as one's self-
    manifestations,
Delusion is purified in a natural way.
Since delusion is purified in this natural way, the Three Bodies
    emerge in their natural arising.
Since the Three Bodies emerge in their natural arising, they
    will have the power to spontaneously perform the good of
    migrating beings.

As to (individuals of) lower capacities,
Even though they have entered the porch of these instructions,
Because of their feeble understanding and realization, they
    have not recognized the Bardo of the Clear-Light of Reality
And are deluded into the karmic Bardo of Becoming.

By the power of these instructions, they will obtain a body in
    fortunate destinies
And, through the purity of their karmic propensities,
They will awaken their previous karmic traces
And will (eventually) obtain liberation within a single birth.

O Son of Noble Clan!
As to the explanation of the way in which delusion (occurs
    because of) nonrealization,
Ordinary individuals who have not entered the porch of these
    instructions
Do not recognize their natural state because of the negative
    power of their karma.

The moving winds (of concepts) arise and agitate the lake of
    Awareness,
Troubled by the ripples of karmic traces and waves of
    discursiveness.

The sky of the Universal Base is covered by the clouds of
    delusion,
While the sun of Awareness is veiled by the darkness of passions.

Sounds, lights, and rays are truly seen as extrinsic manifestations,
And visual manifestations arise as dual because of virtuous and
    sinful karmas.

Endowed with a mental body, (these beings) see it as their past
    form,
And with all complete senses, their mind moves without
    obstacle.

Having no place of support, they also have no protection for
    refuge,
Like children abandoned by their mother.

Enveloped in the darkness of delusion, an ocean of suffering
    wells forth
While they are like fish left behind on hot sand.

The wind of karmic traces rises and they err in the cities of the
    six destinies,
Continuously circling like a water-mill or the wheel of a
    chariot.

How pitiful are these three Realms in which there is no pos-
    sibility for protection!
How exhausting are these fatiguing (rebirths) in which there is
    never any opportunity for liberation!

Think of the flaws of delusion and turn your back to the world!
Generate zeal for the Path, O Fortunate Son of Noble Clan!
Thus the frontier between Buddhahood consecutive to
    realization
And erring in saṃsāra consecutive to nonrealization
Is reached during the bardo; therefore,
This is the key point concerning the way saṃsāra and nirvāṇa
    separate.[127]

127. One would expect here the same literary pattern occurring at the end of the previous chapters, which would be in the context of this last Lamp: *"Thus he spoke.
The Lamp of the Moment of the Bardo is hereby completed. Samaya!" (zhes bya'o/
bar do dus kyi sgron ma rdzogs so/ sa ma ya/).* However, this does not occur in any
of the available editions. This potential line is also missing in the commentaries
by Uri Sönam Gyeltsen and Dru Gyelwa. On the other hand, the following section would have to be considered to be the ultimate part of the sixth chapter, but
since it is a recapitulation of the nature of the entire text, this is rather unlikely.
The absence of the literary pattern mentioned above probably means that the
absence of this pattern in the last chapter was already noticeable in the earliest
versions of the root-text. We will see in the translations of their respective commentaries that Uri Sögyel and Dru Gyelwa used similar versions of the root-text
but not identical ones. There thus already existed variants of the text as early as
the mid-thirteenth century.

Colophon

O Son of Noble Clan!
These six essential points of the Pure and Perfect Mind
Are precepts that lead to realization for those who have not
   (previously) realized their mind; (they are like)
A lamp for those who have no (understanding of the) mind,
A mirror for those who have not seen their mind,
A hook for fleeting minds,
A seal for minds gone astray,
A clarification for dull minds,
An improvement for stiff minds,
A yoke for rigid minds,
And a key for locked minds; because of this,
O Son of Noble Clan,
Evaluate (carefully) in future times if you should impart (these
   teachings) or keep them,
And, in accord with the vessel's faculties,
Guide fortunate individuals on a Path without error!

Thus he spoke.

The Emanation Body (of Tapihritsa) then became invisible,
   like a rainbow disappearing in the sky.
Gurub Nangzher Löpo himself
Decisively ascertained his Awareness and then mastered the
   supreme and manifold ordinary accomplishments.[128]

The Instructions on the Six Lamps of the Great Perfection—
   the Oral Transmission that has not been infiltrated by
   the interpolations of the words of men—are (hereby)
   completed.[129]
May all be auspicious![130]

[ULTIMATE COLOPHON,
ACCORDING TO THE NYARONG PRINT]

Gurub[131] Nangzher Löpo taught it to Phawa Gyelzik Sechung
Who taught it to Mu Tsoge,

---

128. The Kanjur version (vol. 171, p. 229) reads *rdzu 'phrul* (magical displays) instead
    of *dngos grub* (siddhis, accomplishments). The same reading occurs in the Nya-
    rong xylographic print (fol. 16b).

129. The Nyarong xylographic print (fol. 16b) reads: *rdzogs chen sgron ma rdzogs so*
    ("End of the Lamps of the Great Perfection").

130. The colophon of the Dergé xylographic edition of the text is identical.

131. The xylograph reads *gu rug*, but this is a mistake since no clan of this name exists.
    It is rather either *gu rub* or *gu rib*.

Who taught it to Mu Tsotang,[132]
Who taught it to Mu Shötram,
Who taught it to Mu Gyelwa Lodrö,
Who taught it to Pön Tsenpo,[133]
Who taught it to Guge Sherab Loden,
Who taught it to Purong Künga Ripa,[134]
Who taught it to Neljor Sechok,
Who taught it to Lama Khyungji,
Who taught it to Tsi Dewa Ringmo,
Who taught it to Ronggom[135] Tokmé Zhigpo,
Who taught it to Lama Ya-ngelwa.[136]
From him it was gradually transmitted and then handed over
    to me.[137]
Virtue! Virtue! Virtue!

132. Erroneously spelled *stong* (instead of *stang*) in the xylograph. The same spelling occurs in the Ayong Kanjur, vol. 110 f. 21b (see below).

133. He is traditionally regarded as the individual who translated the *Zhangzhung Nyengyü* from its original form in the Zhangzhung language into Tibetan. However, as already noted by Henk Blezer, nothing of the sort can be found in his biography (Blezer, "Greatly Perfected, in Space and Time," p. 87). This must therefore come from another source. Pönchen Tsenpo is also considered the compiler of the root "magic wheels" (*rtsa ba'i 'khrul 'khor*) of the *Zhangzhung Nyengyü*'s yogic training.

134. Otherwise known as Künga Ringmo (Kun dga' ring mo).

135. Erroneously spelled *rang sgom* instead of *rong sgom*.

136. From the colophon of the text included in the Ayong Kanjur, it would appear that this Lama Ya-ngelwa was Dampa Bumjé Ö, the eldest son of Yangtön Chenpo. On the meaning of Ya-ngel as referring to the lamas of the Yang ston clan in Dolpo, see Snellgrove, *The Nine Ways of Bon*, pp. 4–5.

137. I have no explicit information yet as to who this "me" might be. However, from the colophon of the Ayong Kanjur, it would appear that this individual was Ya-ngel Bharu. He is most evidently the same as Ya-ngel Bhasu who appears in the *rGyal gshen ya ngal gyi gdung rabs* (pp. 96–97) as the son of Yangtön Lama Ngakpa (himself the eldest son of Yangtön Tashi Gyeltsen, the younger brother of Dampa Bumjé).

[ULTIMATE COLOPHON, ACCORDING TO THE AYONG KANJUR][138]

Having spoken thusly, the Emanation Body (of Tapihritsa) became invisible, like a rainbow disappearing in the sky. Gyerpung Gurub Nangzher Löpo himself decisively ascertained his Awareness and mastered numerous supernormal powers through his supreme and ordinary accomplishments.

Gyerpung Gurub Nangzher Löpo transmitted (the text) to Phawa Gyelzig Sechung. The latter transmitted it to Mu Tsogé. The latter transmitted it to Mu Tsotong (=Tsotang). The latter transmitted it to Mu Shötrampa. The latter transmitted it to Mu Gyelwai Lodrö. The latter transmitted it to Pön Tsönpo (= Pönchen Tsenpo). The latter transmitted it to Lama Khyungji. The latter transmitted it to Guge Sherab Loden. The latter transmitted it to Purang Künga Ringmo. The latter transmitted it to Neljor Sechok. The latter transmitted it to Khyungji Muthur. The latter transmitted it to Tsi Dewa Ringmo. The latter transmitted it to Ronggom Zhikpo. The latter transmitted it to Lama Yangngel Gongtrawa Chenpo (=Dampa Bumjé Ö).[139] The latter transmitted it to Ya-ngel Bharu. The latter transmitted it to Ya-ngel Töngö.[140] The latter transmitted it to the two

---

138. This colophon has been transliterated in Dan Martin (et al.), *A Catalogue of the Bon Kanjur* (see under text nos. 110–19 of the catalogue).

139. Generally, modern Bönpos identify Ya-ngel Gongtrawa Chenpo with Yangtön Sherab Gyeltsen, but this is a mistake since Gontrawa Chenpo is clearly identified with Dampa Bumjé (Yangtön's eldest son) in the *Nyamgyü*.

140. He was the third son of Ya-ngel Phurpa Kyab (see r*Gyal gshen ya ngal gyi gdung rabs*, p. 100).

Ya-ngal Drangsong.[141] Both transmitted it to Gomchen Sherab Tsültrim. The latter transmitted it to Zhangtön Sönam Rinchen. The latter transmitted it to me.[142]

Moreover, according to another transmission lineage, Lunggom Tokmé requested (the text) from Gongtrawa Chenpo. He then transmitted it to Latö Lama Trülyö.[143] The latter transmitted it to Nyakgom Ringpo. The latter transmitted it to Uring Gomchen. And in the course of the transmission, Gomchen Tönpa (Sherab Tsültrim) requested it from Zhangtön (Sönam Rinchen).

[ULTIMATE COLOPHON ACCORDING TO THE KANJUR MANUSCRIPT OF WELKHYUNG MONASTERY]

These profound oral instructions were gradually transmitted through the six Siddhas of Zhangzhung, such as Phawa Gyeltig (=Gyelzik Sechung),[144] etc., and through the six Trülzhiks,[145]

141. I haven't identified them with certainty at the time of writing this note, but they are probably Tokden Nyakgom and Lama Trülmé. This needs further research and confirmation.

142. The "me" refers to the anonymous author who compiled this colophon.

143. His name should be corrected to Lama Trülmé (Bla ma 'khrul med), a disciple of Ya-ngel Töngö and Tokden Nyakgom (who was also a disciple of Töngö Rinpoche).

144. These were Pawa Gyelzik Sechung, Mushen Tsogé, Gyerchen Tsotang, Mu Shötram Chenpo, Mu Gyelwa Lodrö, and Pönchen Tsenpo.

145. Yogis who have destroyed illusion.

such as Guge Loden, etc.[146] I, Gyeltsen, have requested it from
Segom Yeshe Zangpo.

[ULTIMATE COLOPHON
ACCORDING TO THE SAMLING
MANUSCRIPT][147]

Gurub Nangzher Löpo, having decisively ascertained his Awareness, mastered numerous ordinary and supreme accomplishments.

Gurub Nangzher Löpo transmitted these profound instructions to Phawa Gyeltig (= Gyelzig) Sechung. The latter transmitted them to Mushen Tsogé. The latter transmitted them
to Mu Tsotang. The latter transmitted them to Mu Shötram.
The latter transmitted them to Mu Gyelwa Lodrö. The latter
transmitted them to Pönchen Tsenpo. The latter transmitted
them to Khyungji Muthur. The latter transmitted them to Tsi
Dewa Ringmo. The latter transmitted them to Rong Tokmé
Zhikpo. The latter transmitted them to Lama Ya-ngel Sherab
Gyeltsen. The latter transmitted them to Ya-ngel Bumjé Ö. The
latter transmitted them to Ya-ngel Töngö. The latter transmit-
ted them to Tokden Nyakgom. The latter transmitted them to
Lama Trülmé. The latter transmitted them to Lama Ripa Sherab
Lodrö. From him, (the text) was gradually transmitted to
Gartsa Sönam Lodrö, Pa Tengyel Zangpo, Lopön Trawo Gyelt-

---

146. These were Gugé Shérab Loden, Purang Künga Ringmo, Neldjor Séchok,
     Khyungji Muthur, Tsi Dewa Ringmo, and Ronggom Tokmé Zhikpo.

147. This colophon is similar to, but not exactly identical with, that of the Ayong
     Kanjur.

sen, Sharwa Drangsong Tsültrim Pelzang, Lama Tsawa Gangpa Sherab Özer. From him, my root-master Tokden Rinchen Sherab Gyamtso (received it). And in the presence of the latter, I[148] requested (the transmission), having practiced austerities.

I dedicate all the virtues that have been produced by this copy to the welfare of all sentient beings (whose number) embraces the sky, starting with my benevolent father and mother. May all migrating beings swiftly obtain Buddhahood! May everything be endowed with the principle of auspiciousness! So be it! This was proofread and checked.

---

148. Not identified yet.

PART TWO

COMPLEMENTARY
INSTRUCTIONS

VII. Parallels between the *Six Lamps* and Other Works of the *Zhangzhung Nyengyü*

There exist obvious parallels between the various texts making up the collection of the *Zhangzhung Nyengyü*. They do not constitute overlappings but rather complementary approaches to specific subjects, presented in slightly parallel modes.[149] In fact, as can be seen in the *Method for Teaching the Four Cycles of the Aural Lineage from the Oral Transmission of the Great Perfection in Zhangzhung*,[150] the entire inner, secret, and innermost secret sections of the *Zhangzhung Nyengyü* can be explained and taught according to the basic scheme of the Six Lamps (*sgron ma drug*).[151] Reading the corresponding teachings after the study of each of the six chapters

---

149. On the comparison between the *Six Lamps* and other Bönpo works, such as the *mDzod*, see Blezer, "'Light' on the Human Body," pp. 117–68.

150. *rDzogs pa chen po zhang zhung snyan rgyud kyi bka' rgyud skor bzhi'i 'chad thabs*, Kanjur (A yong *bKa' 'gyur* ed.), vol. 110, pp. 27–54.

151. The expression "Six Lamps" refers here to the subject or theme itself, not to the title of the eponymous text.

of the *Six Lamps* will undoubtedly provide a deeper insight into the meaning of the text itself and enable one to develop a wider understanding of its various themes.

1. TEACHINGS CORRESPONDING TO THE FIRST LAMP

The first Lamp, the Lamp of the Abiding Base (*gnas pa gzhi'i sgron ma*), covers teachings expounded in:

- the first practice of the *Six Essential Points* (*gNad drug*),
- the first chapter of the *Precepts in Eight Chapters* (*Man ngag le'u brgyad pa*), but also in
- the first and second Wheels of the *Four Wheels* (*'Khor lo bzhi*), as well as in
- the first five Seals of the *Twenty-One Seals*.

[1]. The purpose of the first practice of the *Six Essential Points* is to clearly identify the Universal Base (*kun gzhi*). This is done when one is directly introduced to the natural state, and when one clearly discovers the true nature of delusion. The direct introduction to the natural state is given to an individual showing special qualities, such as a natural rejection for saṃsāric activities, devotion to the master, etc. This fortunate individual should remain in an isolated place and perform his practice in total solitariness. He should first take refuge, generate the Pure and Perfect Mind (*bodhicitta*), meditate on impermanence, offer the maṇḍala, etc. Then, on a comfortable cushion, he should apply the key point of the body by remaining in the fivefold posture, controlling his breath and holding it gently, by pressing the upper wind and pulling the lower one. As to the key point of the gaze, the doorways

of the Lamps (the eyes) should be left in their natural state, neither too open nor too closed, the important thing being that the pupils of the eyes remain without moving and clearly focused on the intermediate space (*bar snang*, the atmosphere). For the key point of the mind, the consciousness should be left without grasping at outer objects, analyzing the inner Awareness, or following thoughts of the past and future, etc. Rather, the mind should be left in a state free from any form of grasping. After a while, the pure and impure aspects that are normally affecting the mind will separate from one another and the practitioner will experience the Clear-Light of his own natural state.

Thus when the experience of the knowledge of the natural state arises, one is directly introduced to the nonduality of Clarity and Emptiness. The Mother or Universal Base is introduced as being the unborn Space of the natural state and the Son or Awareness as the luminous Wisdom of this state. The experience of the nonduality of the Mother and the Son (i.e., of Emptiness and Clarity) is the direct introduction to the Absolute Body (*bon sku*). When this experience of the Clarity and Emptiness of the natural state arises in the continuum, the practitioner becomes endowed with a confidence equal to the limitless sky. At that time, it is important to resume the practice according to the way it is explained by Nangzher Löpo in his *Commentary to the Twenty-One Seals*.

According to the practice of the *Six Essential Points*, one should furthermore resolve the nature of delusion by first identifying its causes and conditions, and then by recognizing the actual nature of manifestations associated with delusion. The base of delusion (*'khrul gzhi*) is the nonunderstanding of the nature of the Universal Base and of Awareness. The secondary causes that lead to delusion are expressed in the nonrecognition of the nature of the sounds, rays, and lights. The actual cause of delusion is the incapacity to realize the nature of Awareness. Thus, when the sounds, rays, and lights arise, they are generally not recognized as the expression of the dynamism of Awareness (*rig pa'i rtsal*) and are rather considered outer manifestations separated from ourselves. This is actual delusion (*'khrul pa*). It is compared to the incapacity to recognize one's reflection in a mirror as being one's own reflection and nothing else. By grasping at the three root manifestations (of sounds, rays, and lights) as other induced appearances (*gzhan snang*), the nakedness of Awareness becomes covered with the clothes of conceptual mind, just like the sun is covered by clouds. This incapacity to discern the true nature of the dynamism of Awareness is called "simultaneously born ignorance" (*lhan skyes kyi ma rig pa*), i.e., a form of ignorance that appears simultaneously with the non-recognition of the nature of the three root manifestations. It is because of this ignorance that all the manifestations of delusion occur.

However, in the actual experience of Reality, the Universal Base is similar to the empty sky and Awareness is similar to the atmosphere. This means that there is no base of delusion established by itself: this base of delusion does not exist by itself but appears only because of nonrecognition. When one remains in the actual essence of the Mind, then by applying the oral precepts (*man ngag*) associated with the three root manifestations and by contemplating the related visions, all this appears as self-manifestations (*rang snang*) arising naturally as illusions. At that time one understands that delusion has never occurred, and that it is similar to the death of a child in a dream.[152]

---

152. This image of the death of a child during a dream is even clearer if one does not

[2]. The first chapter of the *Precepts in Eight Chapters* is also concerned with the direct introduction to the natural state of the Mind (*sems nyid*). In this text, Tapihritsa explains that the Absolute Body (*bon sku*) abides in the center of the heart, while the Body of the Transparent Wisdom (*ye shes zang thal gyi sku*) abides in the two eyes. Similarly, the Perfection Body (*rdzogs sku*) abides in the brain, and the Emanation Body (*sprul sku*) abides in the spine. Another Body, that of the Self-Arisen Thiglés (*thig le rang 'byung gi sku*), is presented as abiding in all the channels of the body.

In the course of this initial chapter, Tapihritsa explains that there is no difference between Awareness (*rig pa*) and the Absolute Body (*bon sku*). Awareness radiates in the form of a luminous body (*'od kyi lus*) and abides in a transparent mode that is contemplated through the eyes. This, according to Tapihritsa, constitutes Buddhahood itself, the arising of the Absolute Body endowed with Wisdoms (*ye shes*). At that stage, in the text of the *Eight Precepts*, there is an interlinear note (*mchan*) that summarizes the principles revealed in this chapter. It says:

> In the center of the heart of all sentient beings, the immutable Absolute Body arises as the quintessence of Wisdom that abides as the five clear and vivid Wisdoms. From these five Wisdoms, the five lights come forth, with a Clarity expressed in lights. As to their pure manifestation, these visions of Wisdom arise impartially and abide without declining.[153]

---

have children: their potential death cannot even exist. This is the precise idea behind this simile.

153. See Achard, *The Precepts in Eight Chapters*, p. 44. The authorship of this note

This essence that abides in the center of the heart of all beings is the immutable Essence of Awareness (*rig pa'i ngo bo*) naturally endowed with an unceasing Compassion. The luminous radiance of this Essence manifests without any partiality. It is the Body of Buddhahood (*sangs rgyas kyi sku*) free from elaborations and conceptions, manifesting in the splendors of the fivefold clusters of the Blissful Couples of the five Clans. The natural radiance of this Essence shines in the center of the heart and enters a light channel connecting the heart to the eyes. Therefore, this radiance illuminates the pupils of the eyes and its outer clarity appears in unceasing visions in the sky. This process actually explains the source, path, and dimension of manifestations of the Thögel visions, which are simply the natural radiance (*rang gdangs*) of Awareness. This radiance manifests as Peaceful Bodies (*zhi ba'i sku*) in the heart and as Wrathful Bodies (*khro bo'i sku*) in the Conch Mansion (*dung khang*, the brain), while Emanation Bodies (*sprul pa'i sku*) manifest in the spinal cord. All these Bodies project luminous rays, filling up the entire body of the practitioner, its channels, wheels, etc.

[3]. The first and second Wheels of the Four Wheels have themes that are directly related to the contents of the first Lamp. The first of these Wheels explains in particular the arising of the maṇḍalas of the Three Bodies (*sku gsum gyi dkyil 'khor*), as follows:

---

is unknown to me. It is also clear that it is not always considered a note (or even present either as a note or as a part of the main text) in other versions of the *Eight Precepts*. It is not included in the A yong version of the Kanjur, vol. 110, p. 239a. In the bSam gling manuscript (p. 813), it is included both in the root-text itself and as a dittographic, defective interlinear note. It is clearly integrated in the root-text itself in the edition of the dBal khyung dgon version of the Kanjur (vol. 171, p. 279). The note itself is lacking also in the Nyarong xylographic version (see *gDams pa le'u brgyad pa*, fol. 4b).

Before there arose time limitations and dualities such as saṃsāra and nirvāṇa, the natural state of the Universal Base remained like the sky, free from any partiality. In this space-like state, Awareness arose naturally in the vast expanse of the Base, shining like the sun in the sky. Both Base and Awareness were in a state of nondual perfection, abiding as the nonduality of Space (*dbyings*) and Wisdom (*ye shes*). This corresponds to what is described as the "maṇḍala of the Space of the Absolute Body" (*bon sku dbyings kyi dkyil 'khor*).

Within this nondual Space of the Universal Base and Awareness, the three main manifestations (sounds, rays, and lights) arose spontaneously: the lights displayed themselves in five-fold modes arising as luminous mansions or domes of light; the sounds resonated as the natural sound of Reality throughout the infinite expanse of the Base; and the rays manifested as Thiglés, Citadels, Bodies, etc.

Since these three manifestations are connected to the King of Awareness (*rig pa'i rgyal po*), an unceasing potential of spontaneous arising manifested itself as the maṇḍala of the Perfection Body (*rdzogs sku'i dkyil 'khor*), embracing everything.

Similarly, because of the nondual nature of Space and Wisdom and the unceasing arising of the three main manifestations, various marvels linked to the realization or nonrealization of this state arose in the form of what is designated as the maṇḍala of the Emanation Body (*sprul pa'i sku'i dkyil 'khor*).

The second Wheel describes the circumstances leading to realization (*rtogs*) or delusion (*'khrul*). In this respect, if one realizes that the unceasing potential of manifestations (which is spontaneously accomplished within the state of Awareness) forms our own manifestations (*rang snang*), then this display manifests as nirvāṇa. If one fails to reach such a realization, then one enters the mode of dualistic grasping characterizing saṃsāra.

As to realization, when the three manifestations arise concretely, the mental consciousness recognizes them as its own natural manifestations (*rang snang*) and therefore the state of Awareness is recognized. One does not follow after appearances, thus enabling the King of Awareness to subjugate and gain control over these appearances. At that time, all manifests in fivefold modes that are directly connected to the nirvanic aspect of the natural state, with fivefold lights, Bodies, pure realms, Wisdoms, etc.

On the contrary, when the nature of the three manifestations is not recognized, then one enters the mode of delusion, apprehending sounds, rays, and lights as objects of the intellect (*blo'i yul*). Thus, being mistaken regarding the true nature of these manifestations, one seizes them as endowed with their own characteristics,[154] so that this lack of understanding causes the entrance into dualistic grasping. Then, when the manifestations of delusion arise, they obscure the capacity to realize the true nature of the mind, and because of ignorance, one's consciousness is guided toward objects, grasping at them, analyzing them, etc. At that time, one follows the characteristics of the manifestations and loses control over them, enabling the circumstances leading to saṃsāra to take over. Then, all manifests in fivefold deluded modes, such as vessels (*snod*, i.e., universes), elements, senses, organs, etc. This is how sentient beings come to err within saṃsāra.

Therefore, depending upon the realization or the nonrealization of the nature of the manifestations arising from the Base,

154. As if they had their own inherent existence.

saṃsāra and nirvāṇa arise as marvels coming from the Mind itself, whereas the designations "saṃsāra" and "nirvāṇa" do not exist by themselves but are simply the results of the circumstances leading either to realization or delusion.

[4]. The first five Seals of the *Twenty-One Seals* cover similar subjects associated with the Universal Base (*kun gzhi*), Awareness (*rig pa*), and the mind (*sems*). They are actually more practice oriented, inviting the practitioner to remain in an isolate place in order to be able to easily identify the Universal Base and Awareness. The practice itself is described in its most simple aspects, consisting in sitting in a comfortable position while breathing normally and keeping the eyes without movements. In this pure condition, one should not follow thoughts of the three times. At a certain moment, the experience of Awareness will arise in all its nakedness, and when all discursive thoughts have finally disappeared, one will contemplate the Wisdom (*ye shes*) of the natural state in all its splendor. At that time one will experience the Universal Base, which is (1) without conceptions, (2) the source of everything, (3) neutral, and (4) arising in an unceasing manner. According to the first Seal, it will be easy to cultivate that state by giving up all kinds of distractions and by remaining in the natural ease (*rnal ma*) that characterizes the natural condition of the mind. It is important to be able to cultivate that state without altering it with ordinary thoughts and to become familiar with its dynamism (*rtsal*) in order to reach the Fruit (*'bras bu*) without ever regressing from it.

In the second Seal, Tapihritsa explains that one should train in the practice of sounds, rays, and lights in order to develop visions that are the spontaneous expression of the natural state in its dynamic aspect. At that time it is important to practice in retreat until the Five Visions are reached.[155] The visions arise within the Space of Reality (*bon nyid kyi dbyings*), described in the third Seal as being a synonym of the Universal Base. The visions themselves are the manifestations of the Wisdom of Awareness (*rig pa'i ye shes*) mentioned in the fourth Seal.

Finally, the fifth Seal describes what is known as the Thumb-Sized Absolute Body (*bon sku tshon gang*) or Phalanx of the Dharmakaya. It is an aspect of Wisdom free from limitations, names, colors, etc. This Wisdom is endowed with lights that are not limited to colors or dimensions. It is in fact the Absolute Body itself, the primordial state existing before the advent of Buddhas and sentient beings, saṃsāra and nirvāṇa, etc. This state is known as the Self-Arisen Wisdom (*rang byung ye shes*), free from causes and conditions, beginning or end, etc.

2. TEACHINGS CORRESPONDING TO THE SECOND LAMP

In a similar way, the Lamp of the Flesh-Heart (*tsi ta sha'i sgron ma*) covers teachings corresponding to:

- the second practice of the *Six Essential Points*,
- the second chapter of the *Precepts in Eight Chapters*, and
- the ninth Seal of the *Twenty-One Seals*.

---

155. The Five Visions are a trademark of the *Zhangzhung Nyengyü* teachings.

[1]. In the second practice of the *Six Essential Points*, the text describes how the Base free from obscurations and Awareness free from delusion abide in the practitioner. This actually refers to the sanctuary (*gnas*) where the natural state really abides within ourselves. This sanctuary is known as the Brown Cornelian Tent (*mchong gur smug po*), which is also called Shetün Tsadzin (*she thun rtsa 'dzin*) in the Zhangzhung language, referring to the heart (*tsi tta*).[156]

Even though it is not limited by spatial characteristics, this sanctuary appears outwardly as an eight-cornered jewel and inwardly as an eight-petalled lotus. In its very center abides our own natural state in the mode of the Great Primordial Purity (*ka dag chen po*).

The typical Dzogchen expression referring to this state is "Thumb-Sized Luminous Wisdom" (*gsal ba'i ye shes tshon gang*), described as being similar to a butter-lamp placed within a sealed vase that contains the sounds, lights, and rays arising naturally from this radiating Wisdom.

In order to contemplate the visionary marvels of this state, which is nothing other than Self-Awareness (*rang rig*) itself, one needs to apply the key points of practice, relaxing the doorway of the Lamps and gazing directly into one's own Essence. In this way one will concretely see the natural Clarity of Awareness in its ungraspable mode.

[2]. In the second chapter of the *Eight Precepts*, similar instructions are revealed by Tapihritsa regarding the abiding mode

---

156. On this point, Yongdzin Rinpoche says: "The natural state itself embraces our entire body, speech, and mind, but it is more particularly located within the heart."

of Buddhahood within our own continuum. Basically, the natural state abides within the heart in the mode of Bodies (*sku*) and Wisdoms (*ye shes*) expressing the true essence of our own Awareness. This state manifests itself in the mode of the Three Bodies (*sku gsum*), namely:

- the Absolute Body (*bon sku*) abiding as an unceasing and unobstructed Clarity endowed with Wisdoms displayed in the visions of Awareness,
- the Perfection Body (*rdzogs sku*) manifesting in the form of Buddhas with characteristics of the five clans (*rigs lnga*), etc., and
- the Emanation Body (*sprul sku*) arising in fivefold lights, etc., forming what is known as the marvels of Awareness (*rig pa'i cho 'phrul*).

All the visions contemplated in this way manifest as pervading both the outer Space[157] and the whole of our body, in a transparent (*zang thal*) manner, embracing channels, eyes, consciousness, etc. In this way, the luminous nature of the Buddha within ourselves cannot be obscured by the materiality of the aggregates since it itself manifests in a totally transparent and unblocked mode. The natural radiance of this state located within the heart arises and springs from the eyeballs in a mode enabling the direct contemplation of its visionary displays. As the arising door of Awareness, the eyes are therefore also an important sanctuary of Buddhahood within ourselves.

---

157. This refers to the visionary Space (*dbyings*), not the outer element or atmosphere.

At the time of death, the visions of the natural state will emerge as various lights and, as Awareness springs out from the eyes,[158] it will merge within its own essence as the Absolute Body itself. This constitutes the direct encounter with the Mother (*ma*) or Reality (*bon nyid*). Even during the lifetime, as one is engaged in the main practice (*dngos gzhi*) of Dzogchen, the contemplation of the visions of Bodies and Wisdoms constitutes the direct vision of Buddhahood itself. In this respect, training so as to become familiar with the sounds, lights, and rays through Thögel is the core of Dzogchen practice leading to Buddhahood in this very life.

[3]. In the ninth chapter from the *Twenty-One Seals*, Tapihritsa describes the same sanctuary of Awareness using several similes. The Base (*gzhi*) is thus described as being similar to space and the ocean, in terms of vastness and infinite depths. The lights that naturally rise from this state appear as tents or domes of five-colored rainbows. The sanctuary within our body, hosting that state and its dynamic, visionary displays, is compared to a vase filled with precious jewels. The natural Wisdom manifesting in this state is like a butter-lamp within a vase. The sounds, lights, and rays emerging from this state are like the rays of lights emitted by this lamp.

Thus, according to Tapihritsa, it is crucial to understand that Awareness arises from within, that the Base abides in the mode of Emptiness, that visions arise as the dynamic expression of Awareness itself, and that everything else is nothing but illusions.

---

158. It is its radiance that is arising in this way, Awareness remaining immutable within the sanctuary of the heart.

The abiding mode of Buddhahood within oneself is also described as a celestial Treasure that has been obscured throughout our infinite rebirths in saṃsāra, due to ignorance causing dualistic grasping. This Treasure has no entrance door and therefore its contents cannot be seen like outer material objects. However, upon opening the invisible door of the Treasure (through the actual practice of Thögel), then its innermost contents and visionary marvels are revealed to the practitioner.

3. TEACHINGS CORRESPONDING TO THE THIRD LAMP

As to the Lamp of the White and Smooth Channel (*dkar 'jam rtsa'i sgron ma*), similar teachings are described in:

- the third practice of the *Six Essential Points*,
- the third Wheel of the *Four Wheels*, and
- the tenth Seal of the *Twenty-One Seals*.

There is no corresponding teaching in the *Eight Precepts* though.[159]

[1]. In the *Six Essential Points*, the author comes back to the

---

159. Despite the fact that the teachings of this third Lamp have no parallels in the *Eight Precepts*, instructions regarding the sanctuary of Awareness and its dynamism are of course central themes of the entire secret section of the *Zhangzhung Nyengyü*. See Achard, *The Precepts in Eight Chapters*.

subjects of the sanctuary of Awareness within oneself and of the arising visions forming the dynamic expression (*rtsal*) of this Awareness within the pathway of the channels. The varied nature of the channels explains the variety of the visions of Awareness that one contemplates during practice. The special anatomy that is mentioned in this text describes our main channels and wheels, etc., as follows: "Since there are thus three main channels, six wheels, one trunk, and five main branches, 360 secondary branches, 21,000 minor branches separated into 84,000 leaves and petals, the dynamism of consciousness appears (naturally) manifold."

Therefore, to lower practitioners and ordinary beings, this spontaneous dynamism appears in the mode of erroneous conceptions, while for those who are advanced on the Path, it appears as a continuous flow of experiences and realizations. Furthermore, for those who are fully enlightened, it arises as the spontaneous, impartial, and unceasing dynamism of their own Wisdom (*ye shes*).

The most important of the channels abiding in the body is the channel of the Lamps (*sgron ma'i rtsa*), namely the central channel in which Awareness manifests in its unobstructed mode of Transparent Wisdom (*ye shes zang thal*), the true expression of Emptiness and Clarity.

When one engages in the practice, the winds, mind, and Thiglés are caused to enter and to dissolve within the central channel so that infinite visions of Clear-Light, experiences, and realizations arise. The practice itself is at that time based on the following method: one should sit in the cross-legged posture and pull the stomach against the spine, placing the tongue against the palate and turning the eyes upward. The winds should be pushed downward from the two lateral channels, so as to cause them to enter the central channel itself. At that time, one imagines that the mind and winds are fused into a single Thiglé, which moves upward within the central channel and bursts out through the top of the head. Then, one imagines that this Thiglé is propelled through the infinite sky, like a shooting star, and that it eventually dissolves in the sky, as one keeps one's focus on the outer blue sky. This method is the forceful technique that will enable one to separate the pure Mind from the impure mind and enter directly into the experience of Awareness itself. At that time, one will remain free from the discursive mind and one will experience the dawn of Self-Arisen Wisdom (*rang byung ye shes*).

[2]. In the third chapter of the *Four Wheels*, it is explained that although Awareness embraces the entire body, it is more particularly located within the heart itself. There, its sanctuary is described as an eight-petalled lotus hosting the natural radiance of the five elements. A channel, thin like a white silk thread, connects the heart to the eyes, thus enabling the direct contemplation of Awareness in its visionary marvels (*snang ba'i cho 'phrul*).

In order to illustrate the true abiding mode of the natural state, the texts state that the Universal Base (*kun gzhi*) is like a cloudless sky in which Awareness (*rig pa*) arises as a sun unobscured by darkness. Sounds, rays, and lights (*sgra 'od zer gsum*) are compared to the state of a butter lamp placed within a sealed vase, while mental consciousness arises like the rays of the sun. When all these elements are directly connected to actual practice, one understands that the natural state's sanctuary is the center of the heart, that its pathway is that of the central channel (and more precisely that of the white and smooth channel similar to a silk thread within the central channel), and that its doorways are that of the eyes. As one is directly introduced to the visionary displays of Awareness, one also understands what the base of delusion is, its circumstances, and its essence itself. If, at that time, one realizes that this entire process actually manifests within the natural state itself (and not in a mode existing by itself),[160] then one realizes the actual essence of the Pure and Perfect Mind (*byang chub sems*) and one does not err any longer within the confines of conditioned existence. On the contrary, one will promptly reach liberation without having to pass through the narrow path of the bardo.

[3]. In the tenth chapter of the *Twenty-One Seals*, similar instructions are compiled by Tapihritsa in a more direct style of teaching. There, he says that from the Thumb-Sized Wisdom of Self-Awareness arises a fivefold effulgence displayed in visionary lights. He adds: "From them come the five (original) radiances and from these the five kinds of impurities. The twenty-five (pure and impure elements combined together) generate body and mind."

Awareness manifests itself within the body by pervading the channels (*rtsa*). The central channel is conceived as having an upper section that is the Path of Nirvāṇa, while its lower section is described as the Path of Saṃsāra. The right channel is associated with defects (*skyon*), while the left one is considered to be the channel of Qualities (*yon tan*).

In a further detailed explanation, Tapihritsa states that the central channel is the nondual path of saṃsāra and nirvāṇa, hosting the dynamism of Awareness that thus arises from this pathway. The visions of Awareness then emerge in the empty

---

160. Just like reflections appear in a mirror without altering its surface.

Space of the Universal Base, in various visions of luminous spheres, etc. When the visions of the natural state are contemplated in this way, the text says that "The king of Awareness thus shines nakedly, stripped from the intellectual rags of discursive thoughts." It is at that precise time that one directly sees the true, actual essence of the Self-Arisen Wisdom, free from the darkness of ignorance: with this contemplation, all potential regressions in the saṃsāric mode of conditioned existence are emptied, while the Three Bodies (*sku gsum*) arise naturally by themselves.

4. TEACHINGS CORRESPONDING TO THE FOURTH LAMP

As to the Water Lamp of the Far-Reaching Lasso (*rgyang zhags chu'i sgron ma*), related teachings are expounded in:

- the fourth practice of the *Six Essential Points*,
- the fourth chapter of the *Eight Precepts*, and
- the eleventh Seal of the *Twenty-One Seals*.

[1]. In the fourth chapter of the *Six Essential Points*, the teachings associated with this fourth Lamp—the Water Lamp of the Far-Reaching Lasso—are actually expounded according to two main themes: seeing one's Essence in its nakedness and seeing the visions of Clear-Light in their nakedness.

According to the first of these themes, the direct introduction to one's Essence starts by considering again the location of Awareness within the body, its pathway, and its doorway. Thus, Awareness is described as located in the center of the heart, its pathway being that of the channels, while its arising door (*'char sgo*) is the Water Lamp (*chu'i sgron ma*) itself. Thus, when one remains perfectly stable in the experience of Awareness, the eyes and consciousness remain in their natural condition, without fluctuations. At that time, one can see the Essence of Awareness or experience it as being unborn, luminous, endowed with an infinite Wisdom, etc. The experience that arises at that time is devoid of any limitations and one compares it to the sky free from partialities.[161]

According to the second theme, one should use special means to cause the arising of the visions of Clear-Light in the following manner: one should press the Water Lamps with the fingers and hold the breath. In this way, when visions of lights and rays arise, one contemplates one's own natural radiance and when one releases the pressures of the fingers, one sees fivefold lights, rainbows, etc. Eventually, when one finally exhales the air, one contemplates the visions until they naturally disappear. This is the direct or forceful method applied to cause the direct introduction to the natural dynamism of Awareness (*rig pa'i rang rtsal*).

[2]. In the fourth chapter of the *Eight Precepts*, the main theme is not really that of the fourth Lamp but rather that of the characteristics of the Absolute Body (*bon sku*). But as one shall see, this is not entirely separated from notions dealing with the Water Lamp itself, since it nevertheless insists on the eyes as the sanctuary of the unceasing Clarity (*gsal ba*) of the visions of the Buddhas. These visions are described as arising within the

---

161. This experience is different from the first formless Jhana—known as the "limitless sky" (*nam mkha' mtha' yas*)—in the sense that in the present context, it is endowed with Awareness and Wisdom, which is not the case with the first formless Jhana.

utterly pure Expanse of Reality (*bon nyid kyi klong*) in the form of pure realms expressing the actual Essence of Awareness.

When describing the Absolute Body, Tapihritsa states that it abides as the Single Thiglé (*thig le nyag gcig*) endowed with characteristics. These characteristics are the five Wisdoms (*ye shes lnga*) manifesting the five lights (*'od lnga*). He further says:

"In the center of your heart, the Absolute Body, the Single Sphere, abides as the five Wisdoms (endowed with) the characteristics of the five lights; it abides in the middle of the five lights of the five Wisdoms. These five lights remain vibrant in your heart."[162]

In order to explain how the radiance of Awareness arises as visions at the doorway of the Lamps, he explains that a silk-like channel extends from the center of the heart to the center of the eyes. This channel is supple, devoid of blood and lymph, and only hosts the radiance (*mdangs*) of Awareness itself.

Thus, in the center of the heart, the Absolute Body abides naturally as the five Buddhas endowed with the five Wisdoms and clearly manifesting in an unceasing mode of luminous visions that are contemplated within the sky.[163]

At the same time, the objects of the senses are still being perceived and thoughts are also likely to arise: everything thus arises, expresses itself, and finally dissolves within the state of Awareness. In this context, Tapihritsa anticipates a potential question; he says: "If you think: Is there no distinction between concepts and Wisdom? Are concepts our own Wisdom? (Then

---

162. Achard, *The Precepts in Eight Chapters*, p. 56.

163. These are not objects of the senses, and the sky should be considered merely as a mirror for the reflections of the visions of Awareness. These visions only display as one remains in the natural state and they are not outer sensory objects. This is proven by the fact that they are only contemplated by the practitioner.

know that) when you let your mind (abide) in Reality, you know concepts as being empty, you know that this Emptiness is Reality, and when you know that concepts are Reality, then you reach Buddhahood without duality."[164]

In case one is not able—for whatever outer circumstances—to perfect the entire path of the practice, then at the time of death, the visions of Reality will manifest naturally, and if one is able to recognize this display as one's own Wisdom manifesting in a visionary mode, then one will undoubtedly reach enlightenment at that time.

[3]. Finally, in the eleventh chapter of the *Twenty-One Seals*, Tapihritsa does not only describe the Water Lamp but all the principles centered upon the Wisdom of Self-Awareness (*rang rig ye shes*) as well as the path of visions arising at the doorways of the Lamps. There, he lists four Lamps that differ from the standard presentation of the Four Lamps (*sgron ma bzhi*)[165] and that are here associated with the dispelling of darkness:

- the Water Lamp of the Far-Reaching Lasso (*rgyang zhags chu'i sgron ma*), which dispels mundane darkness,
- the Lamp that manifests Superior Insight (*lhag mthong snang ba'i sgron ma*), which dispels intellectual darkness associated with those who stress a nihilist form of emptiness,

---

164. Achard, *The Precepts in Eight Chapters*, p. 57.

165. The standard list of the Four Lamps enumerates: (1) the Water Lamp of the Far-Reaching Lasso (*rgyang zhags chu'i sgron ma*), (2) the Lamp of utterly pure Space (*dbyings rnam dag gi sgron ma*), (3) the Lamp of Empty Thiglés (*thig le stong pa'i sgron ma*), and (4) the Lamp of the Self-Arisen Sublime Knowledge (*shes rab rang byung gi sgron ma*).

- the Lamp of the Wisdom of Self-Awareness (*rang rig ye shes sgron ma*), which dispels the darkness of ignorance, and
- the Lamp of the Space of the Universal Base (*kun gzhi'i dbyings kyi sgron ma*), which dispels the darkness of the intellect grasping at partialities.

To sum up the process of visionary arising, Tapihritsa states in this Seal:

"The King of Awareness shines in visual perceptions;
It shines in the empty sky of the Universal Base,
In the sheath of visionary lights,
At the doorway of the all-illuminating Lamps;
As a lotus extracting from the mud,
The King of Awareness gushes out from the sheath.
Like the sun free from obscurity,
The King of Awareness is devoid of gloom murkiness.[166]

5. TEACHINGS CORRESPONDING TO THE FIFTH LAMP

Regarding the fifth Lamp, the Lamp of the Direct Introduction to the Pure Realms (*zhing khams ngo sprod kyi sgron ma*), similar teachings are revealed in:

- the fifth, sixth, and seventh chapters of the *Eight Precepts*,

166. Achard, *The Twenty-One Seals*, forthcoming.

- the fifth practice of the *Six Essential Points*, as well as
- the twelfth, thirteenth, fourteenth, fifteenth, sixteenth, and seventeenth Seals of the *Twenty-One Seals*.

[1]. The teachings concerned with the description of the pure realms or visions of Thögel in the fifth chapter of the *Precepts in Eight Chapters* are a natural doctrinal development of the previous instructions dealing with the Base, its abiding mode, its sanctuary, its pathway, and its doorway. When the visions reach a certain level of development, they appear as organized according to the four directions, in a mode corresponding to the natural display of the five Buddhas within the heart with:

- Künnang Khyabpa in the center,
- Selwa Rangjung in the east,
- Ghelha Garchuk in the north,
- Jedrak Ngömé in the west, and
- Gawa Döndrup in the south.

In the Conch Mansion (*dung khang*) are the manifestations of the Wrathful Deities of Wisdom with:

- Tsochok Khangying in the center,
- Trosé in the east,
- Ngamsé in the north,
- Welsé in the west, and
- Tumsé in the south.

In the typical style of the secret cycle of the *Zhangzhung Nyengyü*, Tapihritsa describes the process of visionary arising as follows:

> Since the heart and eyes are connected with a channel and since the eyes are connected with the brain, (owing to the fact that) the assembly of fierce deities supported in the head abides within the brain, their Clarity shines to your own eye-consciousness while they move through your marrow and gush out from the secret door.[167]

In fact, it is the entire maṇḍala of the Peaceful and Wrathful Deities (*zhi khro*) that appears in visionary mode because of the location of these deities within the body. In this respect, what is seen "outwardly" is simply a reflection of what manifests "inwardly."[168] These visions occur when one carefully applies the methods of Thögel practice through its specific key points (*gnad*). In the *Eight Precepts*, Tapihritsa summarizes the process as follows:

> Furthermore, when one opens the door to the Treasury of marvels, the billions of myriad Bodies of Buddhas shine through and this very unceasing Clarity of your Awareness is Full Enlightenment.[169]

---

167. See Achard, *The Precepts in Eight Chapters*, p. 61. See also ibid., p. 105 n. 114, where this secret door (*gsang sgo*) is identified with the Water Lamp according to Shardza Rinpoche's explanations.

168. Of course the distinction between outer and inner is not valid but remains helpful for a conventional explanation.

169. Achard, ibid., p. 62. See also ibid., p. 106.

Opening the Treasury of marvels means applying the methods of Thögel so that the Clarity of Awareness is perceived unceasingly in the celestial visions forming the essence of Awareness. In a stricter sense, and depending on their intensity, these visions pertain to the display of the Perfection and Emanation Bodies (*rdzogs sku* and *sprul sku*).[170]

Similar explanations are given by Tapihritsa at the beginning of the sixth chapter of the *Precepts in Eight Chapters*, where he advises Nangzher Löpo to practice in the following way:

If you wish to see the Body of the Buddha, gaze into the fivefold rainbows! The Buddha is the Body of Transparent Wisdom whose support is in your own body. Its sanctuary abides in the center of (each) eye and its Clarity radiates unceasingly. Recognizing this unceasing Clarity seen by your very eyes is Buddhahood itself.[171]

The beginning of the seventh chapter of the same text contains a synthesis of the previous teachings, which are then put into the context of the instructions for the bardo. At that time, the five lights arise in modes and colors similar to those of rainbows and manifest in the sky before the dying person. At that point, Tapihritsa states:

In the center of these iridescent fivefold lights arise the fivefold clusters of Buddha Bodies filling (Space). Recognizing

170. For a discussion of the visions of the Perfection Body and of the Emanation Body and their parallel with the four actual visions of Thögel, see Achard, *Bönpo Newsletter*, no. 21 (January 2012), p. 3.

171. Achard, *The Precepts in Eight Chapters*, p. 63; see also pp. 107–8.

the Essence of your Self-Awareness as manifesting in the nature of these clusters, you will dissolve within these visions of fivefold clusters and reach Buddhahood without duality.[172]

At that time, the mere realization of this principle is sufficient to liberate from conditioned existence. In this respect, there is strictly nothing to meditate upon, since recognizing this visionary reality of the natural state is liberating in itself.

[2]. In the fifth chapter of the *Six Essential Points*, the practice of the Path is combined with the complete elucidation of the nature of the Three Bodies (*sku gsum*). It is structured around successive direct introductions (*ngo sprod*) followed by clarifications and by a condensed description of the actual practice itself.[173] In this text, previous instructions are given for the context of dark retreats (*mun mtshams*), but here they actually describe the sky-gazing technique, which has similar key points such as:

- the key point of the body (*lus kyi gnad*), referring to postures (like those of the Lion, Elephant, Sage, etc.),
- the key point of the senses (*dbang po'i gnad*), referring to appropriate gazes (upward, sideward, and downward),
- the key point of breath (*rlung gi gnad*), consisting in breathing through the mouth, without blocking, and

172. Ibid., p. 65.

173. The details of the practice are to be found in the *Chaktri* set of instructions. The most fascinating explanations on this practice published so far in English are two volumes by Yongdzin Rinpoche (ed. by Gerd Manusch) entitled: *The Main Dzogchen Practices* and *The Meditation on the Clear-Light*. See the bibliography for full references. They provide the practitioner with extensive explanations on how to conduct the practice of Clear-Light (*'od gsal*) itself.

- ◆ the key point of the mind (*sems kyi gnad*), consisting in letting the mind contemplate the visions of Awareness, without visualizations, projections, etc.

When one trains correctly while applying these key points, one will see the visions of Clear-Light display like the multitude of stars illuminating the sky. At that time, the practice will progress through the five following Visions (*snang ba lnga*):[174]

- ◆ the Increasing of Visions (*snang ba 'phel ba*),
- ◆ the Spreading of Visions (*snang ba mched pa*),
- ◆ the Intensification of Visions (*snang ba rgyas pa*),
- ◆ the Perfection of Visions (*snang ba rdzogs pa*), and
- ◆ the Ultimate Stage of Visions (*snang ba mthar thug*).[175]

Each of them is divided into "outer" visionary experiences (*snang nyams*) and "inner" sapiential experiences (*shes nyams*). It is interesting to note that the text here says:

As to the time necessary to reach that ultimate limit,
Superior practitioners will do so in seven days,
Intermediate practitioners will do so in twenty-one days, and
Ordinary practitioners will reach this ultimate limit in one month and ten days.

174. These constitute an exclusive characteristic of the *Zhangzhung Nyengyü* in which the standard second Vision of Thögel is divided into two visionary stages.

175. The details regarding these visions are given in Yongdzin Rinpoche, *The Meditation on the Clear-Light* (ed. Gerd Manusch).

This clearly applies to the best practitioners among the best (*rab kyi rab*), to the medium among the best (*rab kyi 'bring*), and to the lower among the best (*rab kyi tha ma*). It should be noted that it took Tapihritsa nine years in complete solitude to reach that ultimate stage, a remark that is a good reference to measure one's own level and avoid fantasizing about contemplating a couple of translucent Thiglés. The duration to which the text refers concerns highly advanced practitioners only. In conclusion of this section, the text of the *Six Essential Points* says:

> Thus, one should understand that all that arises, such as the sounds, rays, and lights, the threads of Thiglés, the Form Bodies and their Citadels, the pure realms, maṇḍalas, etc., are the arising mode of the dynamism of Awareness, and one should have in mind the certainty that they are devoid of inherent nature.

[3]. In Seals twelve and thirteen, the visions of Awareness arising during the practice of Thögel are described as the spontaneous dynamism of Awareness itself and as forming the maṇḍala of the Three Bodies. In this respect, the twelfth Seal says:

> The Absolute Body, which is self-Awareness, emerges from the expanse of the heart;
> The Body of natural Perfection stands in the pathway of the channels; and
> The Emanation Body emerges naturally at the doorway of the Lamps.

In a similar way, the next Seal says with more details:

The five visionary lights are the Base of the pure realms
    maṇḍalas,
The tents of luminous spheres are the Citadels of the Five
    Clans,
On the Bodies of Superior Insight emerges a multitude of
    Form Bodies,
The threefold union is the emanation Base of the Three
    Bodies (while)
The fivefold deities, Bodies, Clans, Wisdoms,
Couples of main (deities) and their entourage are emana-
    tions that cannot be fathomed by thought.

To synthesize the entire perspective given in the text, Tapihritsa
states in Seal fourteen: "All this is perfected within the Single
Thiglé." This means that everything occurs within the natural
state, expresses itself within that state, and eventually dissolves
within that state. This is the very reason why this natural state
is designated as the "Single Thiglé" (*thig le nyag gcig*) in typical
Dzogchen terminology.

When one reaches the ultimate stage of visionary practice,
one enters the level of exhaustion (*zad sa*) in which everything
dissolves back into the natural state: everything gradually resorbs
in the primordial state until there is only the empty luminous
Space of Reality. This condition is however not nihilistic, since it
is endowed with a potential or dynamism (*rtsal*) likely to let various emanations arise, such as pure realms (*zhing khams*), in order
to host our Emanation Bodies for the sake of sentient beings, etc.
Before that, Tapihritsa describes the end of the exhaustion stage,
saying that "sounds, lights, and rays dissolve into the Space of
Awareness and the entirety of saṃsāra and nirvāṇa dissolves into
the Mind of Perfect Purity." He adds in conclusion:

This exhaustion of manifestations is not the cessation of nihilism: their source of arising and their ultimate liberation meet here (since) these inexhaustible and ceaseless (marvels) never end.

6. TEACHINGS CORRESPONDING TO THE SIXTH LAMP

Finally, as to the sixth Lamp, the Lamp of the Moment of the Bardo, similar teachings are covered in:

- the eighth chapter in the *Precepts in Eight Chapters*,
- the fourth Wheel in the *Four Wheels*, and
- the eighteenth and nineteenth Seals of the *Twenty-One Seals*.

[1]. The last section of the *Precepts in Eight Chapters* is concerned with the teachings explaining "the manner in which practitioners of best, medium, and ordinary capacities liberate in the narrow path of the intermediate state."[176] The overall process of visionary arising is first synthesized by Tapihritsa, who condenses in a few lines the teachings he revealed in the previous chapters of this text. In this respect, he explains that the Essence of our own Awareness abiding in the heart is the Buddha itself, which manifests in a mode totally free from birth and death, production and cessation. Experiencing that unceasing recognition is the Contemplation of the Buddha (*sangs rgyas kyi dgongs*

176. Achard, *The Precepts in Eight Chapters*, p. 65 ff.

pa). In its nature abiding as free from physical characteristics, this Body manifests as the Transparent Wisdom (*ye shes zang thal*) that cannot be obstructed by anything. The visions that are being manifested through the dynamism of this Wisdom arise as the five lights displayed in increasingly complex mandalic forms.

At the time of death, Awareness comes forth through the eyes and manifests its natural radiance displayed in lights and Bodies. If this is recognized as one's own manifestations (*rang snang*), then saṃsāra is overcome and all deluded appearances arise as Wisdoms. At that time, one reaches the ultimate stage of Primordial Purity (*ka dag*) and obtains full Buddhahood.

The yogis of highest capacities achieve Buddhahood at the end of the Path, without leaving residual aggregates behind them. Those of intermediate capacities reach that stage at the moment when body and mind part from one another. And those of ordinary capacities are likely to reach Buddhahood during the intermediate state.

[2]. More explicit instructions are given in the last chapter of the *Four Wheels*, where the modes of liberation (*grol tshul*) of the three categories of practitioners are described as follows:

Those of higher capacities reach Buddhahood during their lifetime without experiencing the postmortem bardo states. No further elements are given in terms of practice or in terms of the manifestation of the Fruit of these yogis.

The teachings are particularly detailed for the yogis of intermediate level. It is said that they will reach Liberation during the course of the Bardo of Clear-Light (*'od gsal gyi bar do*). At that time, the outer manifestations of the four main elements—fire, water, earth, and air—cease and the manifestations of sounds, lights, and rays arise. At the time of death, their mind separates from the body and abides without support. At that time, all manifestations appear as lights, as fivefold pure realms, etc. Rays appear as colorful, indeterminate marvels, while sounds reverberate as the natural sound of Reality, similar to the unceasing roar of thunder. Those who have become familiar with the visions of the natural state during their lifetime will on this occasion contemplate the visions of Bodies (*sku*) and full maṇḍalas manifesting in their total perfection. At that time, the mental body projected by the consciousness will appear luminous and still without face or back. Infinite numbers of luminous tents or domes will arise in the ten directions of the sky, filled with fivefold maṇḍalas, etc.

At that time, one shall reach liberation after the arising of the six foreknowledges and the six rememberings. The six foreknowledges are:

- knowing past and future lives,
- knowing the causes and results of karma,
- knowing pure and impure realms,
- knowing the Bardo of the Clear-Light of Reality,
- knowing that sounds, rays, and lights are our own manifestations, and
- knowing or recognizing the natural state of our own Awareness in a manifest manner.

The six rememberings are:

- remembering that one has just passed away,
- remembering that one is in the bardo,
- remembering that one's mind has no physical support anymore,

- remembering the nature of the visions appearing at that time,
- remembering the master, and
- remembering the instructions on the Yidam given by the master.

Basing oneself on the oral instructions received during the lifetime, one also remembers that sounds, lights, and rays are our own manifestations and consequently one remembers the actual nature of one's own Awareness. At that time, one directly contemplates the "face" of the King of Awareness while ignorance and delusion are naturally purified. The Three Bodies (*sku gsum*) arise consequently, in a natural emergence (*rang shar*) through which one can strive for the benefit of all beings.

As to practitioners of lower capacities, who have not been able to reach Buddhahood during their lifetime, at the time of death or during the Bardo of Clear-Light, they are confronted with the Bardo of Becoming (*srid pa'i bar do*), during which the power of their positive actions will help them obtain a body in a favorable destiny. After an ultimate rebirth, they will reach liberation and manifest the realization of the Three Bodies.

Ordinary beings who have not received and practiced these oral instructions will not recognize the sounds, rays, and lights as their own manifestations and will enter dualistic confusion. Their only possibility of rebirth will be in conditioned existence, mostly among the lower realms.

[3]. Tapihritsa expounds similar instructions in the eighteenth and nineteenth chapters of the *Twenty-One Seals*. In the first of these two chapters, he states that at the time of death, practitioners of highest capacities are given instructions on the natural

arising of Wisdom, in order to refresh their mind regarding the teachings they have practiced during their lifetime. Those of intermediate capacities are given instructions on nonattachment and nongrasping at the manifestations appearing at the time of death and in after-death states. In this way, they should be able to cut off the doors of lower rebirths and, according to their own individual level, gain liberation or a favorable rebirth. Finally, those of lower capacities are given teachings about the Yidam and the master, and they are taught instructions on devotion to the master and aspiration for a rebirth in a favorable destiny or realm.

In the next Seal, Tapihritsa covers teachings that complement those he has given in the last chapters of the *Six Lamps* and of the *Eight Precepts*. He states that at the time of death, one is in a situation of potentially attaining liberation (*grol*) or experiencing again delusion (*'khrul*). At the precise time of death, the elements dissolve into their own place and dualistic grasping is absorbed into the vast Expanse (*klong*) of the Universal Base, together with all discursive thoughts. It is thus a perfect occasion to recognize that Awareness abides in its total nakedness and that nothing obscures it anymore.

If they fail to recognize that with certainty, then individuals are confronted with the first bardo.[177] At that time, lights arise as pure realms, sounds reverberate within the pure Expanse of Reality, and rays manifest in an infinite variety of visionary marvels similar to unfolded silk brocade.

---

177. Tapihritsa considers here only the postmortem bardo and refers in this context to the Bardo of the Clear-Light of Reality. The Bardo of the Primordially Pure Absolute Body (*ka dag bon sku bar do*) is not discussed in the corpus of the *Zhangzhung Nyengyü*.

Those who have trained in Thögel practice during their lifetime but who have failed to perfect the Path in its entirety and are therefore confronted with the bardo states will see Bodies and various maṇḍalas appear in all directions. Through the manifestation of the six foreknowledges and six rememberings listed above, they will recognize that all the visions appearing at that time are simply the natural display of their own Awareness. All forms of ignorance and delusions will be naturally purified and the three Realms of Saṃsāra will be stirred to their very depths. The maṇḍalas of the Three Bodies will natural arise and liberation will be obtained without doubt.

Those of lower familiarization with the natural dynamism of the primordial state will remain unconscious for a duration of one to three days. Consequently, they will not be able to contemplate the splendors of the pure realms in their total perfection and they will be confronted with the Bardo of Becoming. Still, at that stage, they have the possibility to take a rebirth in a favorable place (like a pure realm, etc.) where they will be able to follow teachings and eventually reach Buddhahood.

Ordinary beings will not recognize anything during that time. They will grasp dualistically at the visions and enter again the trap of delusion, leading to a further wandering into saṃsāra.

Parallels are also to be found regarding the final conclusion of the *Six Lamps*, which covers similar information shared in the last chapter of the *Twenty-One Seals*, as well as in the conclusion of the *Precepts in Eight Chapters* and in the *Non-Action Devoid of Traces* (*Bya bral rjes med*).

Such parallels and common themes exemplify the internal coherence of the *Zhangzhung Nyengyü* instructions, which complement each other in the form of a multifaceted mirror-like jewel. The "methods for teaching" (*'chad thabs*)[178] were traditionally used during transmissions of the entire *Zhangzhung Nyengyü* and for gradually guiding individuals in their meditation during specific retreats. Teachings would thus be transmitted in a progressive way and the related chapters in the other texts of the collection were studied concurrently. Such methods are unfortunately rarely used nowadays, but this is the traditional way the teachings should be given.

178. Two such texts have found their way into the Ayong edition of the Kanjur (see Dan Martin et al., *A Catalogue of the Bon Kanjur*, nos. 110-1 and 110-2) but are surprisingly absent from all other editions of the *Zhangzhung Nyengyü*, even recent ones that, on the other hand, include extra works such as Shardza Rinpoche's *Great Primordial Consecration* (*Ye dbang chen mo*) and other texts, not traditionally listed as belonging to the cycle.

VIII. The Complementary Works to the *Six Lamps*

The cycle of the *Instructions on the Six Lamps* can be divided into the following five parts or inner sections: (1) the root-text itself, (2) the commentaries, (3) the actual complementary works, (4) further doxographical works, and (5) the practice manual.

1. THE ROOT-TEXT

The root-text of the *Instructions on the Six Lamps* is described by the later tradition as the transcription of Tapihritsa's teachings made by Gyerpung Nangzher Löpo, most certainly a short time after his meeting with Tapihritsa. The circumstances are given in the preface and complemented by the scanty information recorded in the colophon. If we accept this at face value, then it would mean that the text originated most certainly in Zhangzhung or Western Tibet, sometime during the eighth century, Nangzher Löpo being presented in the *Reasons Why Bön Was Not Abolished* (*Bon ma nub pa'i gtan tshigs*) as a contemporary of

Emperor Trisong Detsen (755–97). So far, no version of the *Six Lamps* dating to that time has been found, at least to my knowledge. Rather, it would seem that the teachings of the *Six Lamps* appear on the historical scene of the Bön tradition sometime around the late tenth–early eleventh century. Still we have to my knowledge no version dating to that period either, but the early eleventh century is the time when Dampa Bumjé Ö (the eldest son of Yangtön Sherab Gyeltsen) was active in the Dolpo area. He is credited with the composition or collection of instructions that are compiled in the *Six Essential Points of Pure and Perfect Mind* (*Byang chub sems kyi gnad drug*, on which see sections 3–5 below). Since this work draws heavily from the *Six Lamps*, it logically follows that the text of the *Six Lamps* existed before Dampa Bumjé started his own *Six Essential Points*.[179] Therefore, regarding the dating of the *Six Lamps*, one can say that:

- traditionally, it is ascribed to the eighth century, and
- academically, it dates at least from the eleventh century and may certainly be earlier than that.

The contents of the text can also shed some light on its history. The style of the text itself is unlike that of the royal period, which therefore does not sustain its high antiquity. It is clearly presented in a stylistic manner that is obviously of regular, literary written standards but that also shows a definite "oral style," which would sustain the way its history is traditionally presented. Therefore, there are great chances that this work carries

---

179. On other texts that may have contributed to the *Six Lamps* in its written form, see the recent, illuminating research work by Blezer in "'Light' on the Human Body" (see the bibliography for full reference).

instructions that were probably given in an oral mode at one time or another and that were put into written form at a later time. As can be seen by the structure of the root-text, this work is more complex than it actually looks after a quick glance. Each chapter is divided into (1) a concise presentation (*mdor bstan pa*), (2) a detailed explanation (*rgyas par bshad pa*), and (3) a conclusion (*mdor bsdus pa*).

The section concerned with the detailed explanation can be subdivided into as many subjects as demanded by the contents themselves. This is a rather traditional, exegetical approach, which was current since the royal period but which is probably unlikely to be found in a theoretically genuine "oral teaching," especially if not based on a written source used for the exegesis itself.

Given these elements, I would for the time being conclude that the root-text itself is most certainly based on oral teachings (as shown by the style of some sections of the text) that have been later arranged for exegetical purposes and systematized according to a scheme that aims at pointing to three main doctrinal elements:

- philosophical teachings on the nature of the Universal Base (*kun gzhi*), Awareness (*rig pa*), and mind (*sems*), as well as the mode of liberation (*grol tshul*) and the mode of delusion (*'khrul tshul*);
- anatomical teachings on the sanctuary of the natural state within the body, its pathway, and its arising door; the teachings on the visionary nature of this state in the visions of Thögel should be considered the link between the visions arising during the lifetime and those arising after death; and

- explanatory teachings on the visions specifically arising at the time of death and after death, followed by
  the modes of liberation of practitioners according to
  their spiritual level.

Thus, the contents of the text itself can be summed up to three
main themes, which form the core of standard Dzogchen
teachings:

- instructions on the natural state of the mind, described
  as Trekchö (*khregs chod*) teachings in other cycles;
- instructions on its visionary expression, described as
  Thögel (*thod rgal*) teachings elsewhere; and
- bardo teachings dealing with mortem and postmortem
  states.

2. THE COMMENTARIES

There are to my knowledge only two commentaries to the root-
text. Their very existence is a problem in itself: according to
modern Bönpos, it is forbidden to write commentaries to the
root-texts of the *Zhangzhung Nyengyü*.[180] However, there is
not a single word about this rule in the root-texts of the *Kagyü
Korzhi* itself. Such a rule is to be actually found several times
within the texts of the Experiential Transmission (*Nyams rgyud*)

---

180. The *Zhangzhung Nyengyü* itself in its latest edition (Gangs ti se bon gzhung)
   contains a total of 32 texts, 18 of which are of a complementary or commentato-
   rial nature, leaving 14 texts that only are, without doubt, root works from which
   the others were elaborated.

and in particular in the long and medium versions.[181] This rule is in fact contradicted by the actual existence of these two commentaries, which, if the rule existed at the time of the composition of these two works, would be in a very ambiguous situation within the tradition, rather than enriching it.[182]

What was true and valid for Nangzher Löpo in the eighth century proved to be valid for masters like Uri Sönam Gyeltsen and Dru Gyelwa (the two main commentators) in the thirteenth century *in the very same way* and literary context as in the eighth century. There is no reason to change things according to time since the same rules must apply to present-day situations. Therefore, as I have discussed with Yongdzin Rinpoche, introducing comments in oral mode that are then transcribed into written form constitutes a transgression of the rule.[183] But this problem goes one step further: conditioning the teachings to the audience actually leads to a dramatic result. Since the audience is rarely, if ever, at the level of understanding properly the

181. There is no need to remind the reader here that the texts of the Experiential Transmission were codified by Yangtön Sherab Gyeltsen and later by his eldest son in the late eleventh century. Therefore they are in theory later than the root-texts of the *Zhangzhung Nyengyü* itself.

182. But it is also contradicted by many "oral teachings" given throughout the history of the collection and best exemplified by the contemporary situation. We are indeed confronted these days with, on the one hand, actual oral instructions associated with the root-texts of the cycle as exemplified by the canonical teaching activities of Yongdzin Rinpoche in exile (but also by several contemporary masters very active in Tibet), and on the other hand, teachings given by so-called masters who contextualize the instructions according to their audience and who thus transgress the rule by adding contextual explanations to instructions that are beyond such conditioning factors.

183. It is not the oral commentary that is to be questioned but the transcription of the teachings that form a written exegetical composition in blatant contradiction with the rule established in the *Nyamgyü*.

actual teaching,[184] then the teachings are lowered to the level of this audience and therefore the result is not Dzogchen teachings but a simplification. In this perspective, a simplified teaching entails a simplified understanding, which is brought into an individual's simplified practice, leading to nothing else than a simplified result. That result is a direct return to delusion (*'khrul pa*).

For this reason, and given the fact that the actual collection of the *Zhangzhung Nyengyü* is replete with commentaries, one must admit that this rule is most certainly valid for the texts of the Experiential Transmission but is overwhelmingly contradicted by the literary existence of commentaries on the root-texts of the *Kagyü Korzhi*. Moreover, if it were not for the existence of the two commentaries on the *Six Lamps*, I doubt that the exegetical level reached by the oral explanations of the root-text would match the actual intent of the original compiler of the text itself.

The proof of this last argument is actually demonstrated by the fact that nearly all transmissions of the *Six Lamps* that I was able to witness during the past twenty-five years in Tibet or in the West were entirely based on one of the two existing commentaries, with a marked preference for Dru Gyelwa's version.

The first commentary, the *Commentary on the Lamps known as the Ornament of Solar Lights* (*sGron 'grel nyi 'od rgyan*), is generally thought to predate that of Dru Gyelwa Yungdrung

---

184. This lack of understanding does not depend on the intellectual capacities of the members of the audience, who generally have an education level above the standards of Tibetan educational systems, but rather on the fact that they are regularly taught "light" versions of the teachings and very rarely the actual texts themselves. The problem thus entirely lies on the shoulders of those who "teach" in a mode that does not reflect the actual contents of the texts but rather an adaptation, which, provided this situation keeps on, is going to play a tragic role in the disappearance of the original teachings in the very near future.

(1242–1290). It is attributed to Uri Sönam Gyeltsen, who was apparently an older contemporary of Dru Gyelwa.[185] The latter's commentary is entitled the *Commentary on the Contemplative Meaning of the Six Lamps* (*sGron ma drug gi dgongs don 'grel pa*) and shows a more systematic approach in its commentarial form, which is certainly the reason why this second commentary is more widely used during oral transmissions.[186]

3. THE ACTUAL COMPLEMENTARY WORKS

Within the *Zhangzhung Nyengyü* itself, there are four works that can be classified among the actual complementary texts to the *Six Lamps*. Their themes cover subjects that are discussed in the root-text but that are presented in a more developed manner. This is the case, for instance, for the first of these four works, namely the *Lamp Clarifying the Oral Advice on the Universal Base* (*Kun gzhi zhal shes gsal ba'i sgron ma*). This text explains the notion of Universal Base (*kun gzhi*) as it should be understood in the context of the *Zhangzhung Nyengyü* teachings in general, and in the context of the *Six Lamps* in particular.

It is a subject that has caused a lot of polemical literature, mostly because those attacking Dzogchen fail to understand the difference between the Universal Base (*kun gzhi*) as it is explained in Dzogchen texts and the consciousness of the

---

185. Yangtön Pelzang, however, attributes this commentary to Nyaktön Ripa Shertsül (Sherab Tsültrim), Uri's root master. See also Blezer, "Greatly Perfected," p. 92.

186. I discuss the structure and contents of these two commentaries in the introduction to their respective translations, forthcoming.

Universal Base (*kun gzhi rnam shes*) as it is explained in Cittamatra literature (as well as in Dzogchen, for that matter). If the consciousness of the Universal Base is the same in both traditions, Dzogchen's unique conception is that of the Universal Base (*kun gzhi*) itself in which "Universal" (*kun*) does not refer to an ocean-like consciousness but rather to the fact that, depending upon the realization of its manifestations (*snang ba*), the Base manifests as that of saṃsāra or that of nirvāṇa. In the first case, it becomes the base for delusion (*'khrul gzhi*), while in the second it is the Base of Liberation (*grol gzhi*).

The text of the *Lamp Clarifying the Oral Advice on the Universal Base* is itself divided into eight sections using different similes to explain the nature of that Base. The first four similes explain how to clearly understand the way in which the natural state embraces beings; these similes are those of (1) the outer sky and the inner sky; (2) the moon and the water-moon (*chu zla*, or reflection of the moon into the water); (3) further explanations about the water-moon (*chu zla*) and the Single Thiglé (*thig le nyag gcig*); and (4) a castle and its various doors.

The first simile is used to explain why Awareness (*rig pa*) or the natural state embraces everything. This is aimed at showing that actually nothing "exists" outside the natural state, a statement that is different from saying that everything *has* a natural state.

It is in this section of the text that objects are clearly defined as inert matter (*bem po*) devoid of Awareness. Therefore, those acknowledging a wrong definition of "Pervading Awareness" (*khyab rig*) are demonstrated as heretics lacking the capacity to understand what Rigpa and the natural state are.

The second simile provides an even clearer demonstration about the wrong understanding of Awareness affecting minds that are not favored by the intelligence of actual penetration of the real meaning of the natural state. I will paraphrase the text as follows:

When the moon shines in space, its light arises in a mode embracing the whole of the earth. Therefore, since the inherent clarity of rivers, ponds, and lakes is *a priori* pure, they possess a ground that enables the arising of water-moons (*chu zla*, reflections of the moon within water), and consequently the reflections of the moon appear upon them.

On the other hand, insofar as the soil, stones, and rocks are opaque, they lack such a ground for the arising of water-moons. Thus, even if the light of the moon embraces them, not a single reflection of the moon appears upon them.

In the same way, just like the maṇḍala of the moon shines over everything, the natural state embraces the entirety of saṃsāra and nirvāṇa, but only inner Awareness has the power to realize such a state because it possesses a potential or ground that enables the arising of the realization of Reality, in the same way that water has the potential to reflect the image of the moon.

The manifestations of outer objects, as well as entire universes, etc., are material things devoid of Awareness, and therefore they don't possess any ground or potential for the arising of the realization of Reality, even though they are embraced by Awareness. Therefore, such inert objects cannot realize Awareness, experience it, or be endowed with it.

For this reason, the few modern deluded individuals advocating that objects have an Awareness are to be considered vessels filled with the poison of wrong views (*log lta*). Such wrong views are based on a wrong understanding of what Awareness is, how it functions, and what its qualities are. This is why actual, real Dzogchen teachings should be kept secret from such persons.

The four last sections of the text respectively deal with (5) the way karmic traces are accumulated (using the example of a household with a husband, wife, etc.); (6) the image of the mirror with its potential for reflections; (7) the example of dreams; and (8) instructions dealing with the bardo states.[187]

The second of the complementary works is the *Setting of the Four Wheels* (*'Khor lo bzhi sbrag*), which has been summarized by Samten Karmay in his *Little Luminous Boy*. I will just remind the reader of the structure of this text, which is composed, as its title indicates, of four Wheels (*'khor lo*) or chapters dealing with (1) the Abiding Base (*gnas pa gzhi*), (2) interdependent origination (*rten 'brel*), (3) the key point of the body (*lus gnad*) and channels (*rtsa*), and (4) the moment of the bardo (*bar do dus*).

The third among the complementary works is the *Non-Action Leaving No Traces* (*Bya bral rjes med*), which has an opening narrative similar to that of the *Six Lamps* but in fact appears to be closer to earlier narratives that are included in the first section of the *Zhangzhung Nyengyü*.[188] Next, are included the teachings

---

187. As mentioned earlier, there exists a French translation of the root-text with two commentaries based on oral transmissions and teachings. See the bibliography for full references.

188. These narratives are described here as "earlier" because they are supposed to have

that Tapihritsa is said to have transmitted to Nangzher Löpo on the occasion described in the opening narrative itself. These instructions are divided into:

+ the Non-Action of the Abiding Base (*gnas pa gzhi'i bya bral*),
+ the Non-Action of the Path to be entered (*'jug pa lam gyi bya bral*), and
+ the Non-Action of the ultimate Fruit (*mthar phyin 'bras bu'i bya bral*).

The teachings are then discussed according to three kinds of explanatory methods (*bshad lugs rnam pa gsum*), namely:

+ the explanation of the primordial Thusness (*ye ji bzhin mar bshad pa*),
+ the explanation applied to the natural state (*gnas lugs dang sbyar te bshad pa*), and
+ the explanation applied to the mind of the individual (*gang zag blo dang sbyar te bshad pa*).

These are, however, not extensively described in the text, which then goes on to explain the proper meaning of "Non-Action" (*bya bral*) and "Absence of Traces" (*rjes med*) in an exegetical manner that looks as if some commentarial exegesis had been introduced into the text. In the last part of the work, the

---

happened during the first meeting of Tapihritsa and Nangzher Löpo. They are to be found in three related texts: the *Prophecies of Lord Tapihritsa* (*rJe ta pi hri tsa'i lung bstan*), the *Nine Homages* (*Zhe sa dgu phrug*), and the *Second Meeting* (*mJal thebs bar ma*). These works have been translated with commentary in Achard, *Les Prophéties de Tapihritsa*, Editions Khyung-Lung, 2005.

unknown author or compiler explains that, upon receiving the Contemplation of the Buddha (*sangs rgyas kyi dgongs pa*), Gyerpung Chenpo obtained realization in a single day, after which Tapihritsa explained to him the different kinds of liberating experiences (*nyams*) that are likely to occur when the oral instructions of the lineage have been clearly integrated by a practitioner. Final exhortations to look at one's mind, to subjugate the five poisons, and to let them arise as the five Wisdoms, etc., conclude this treatise.

The fourth among the complementary texts is that of the *Six Luminous Spheres* (*Thig le drug pa*). This is clearly a reworking of the text of the *Six Lamps* itself without the narrative and with a different opening structure. It includes a section entitled "The Root Verses of the Six Luminous Spheres" (*thig le drug pa'i rtsa tshig*), which can be rendered as follows:

> In the Thiglé of the abiding Basis,
> One is introduced to the arising mode of Awareness.
> If one is not introduced to the Base,
> The base of delusion will not be cut from its roots.

> In the Thiglé of the Flesh-Heart,
> One is introduced to the abiding mode of Awareness
> And if one does not practice accordingly,
> The actual natural state of the Mind will not be clearly
> ascertained.

> In the Thiglé of the White and Smooth Channel,
> One is introduced to the pathway of Awareness.
> If one does not recognize this pathway,

The purity of Awareness will not be distinguished from
   impurity.

In the Thiglé of the Far-Reaching Lasso that illuminates
   (everything),
One is introduced to the signs of Awareness.
If this is not illustrated symbolically with the eyes that illumi-
   nate (everything),
Then the Clear-Light will not be clearly ascertained.

In the Thiglé of the direct introduction to the pure realms,
One is introduced to the archetype of Awareness.
If this is not illustrated symbolically as such an archetype,
The mental proliferations regarding Thiglés will not be
   eradicated.

In the Thiglé of the moment of the bardo,
The dissolution and transfer of Awareness are explained.
Such are the Root Verses of the Six Thiglés.[189]

As one can see from these verses, the contents discussed in these
Six Luminous Spheres follow the very same subjects as those discussed in the *Six Lamps*. However, the texts are of course not
identical but rather complement each other.[190]

---

189. The Nyarong version of the text has slightly different verses in several cases (pp.
   193–94). I have followed the Ayong Kanjur version, which is, however, often
   faulty in many of its readings.

190. One can note, for instance, that the *Six Luminous Spheres* does not use the concept of Universal Base (*kun gzhi*) in its explanation of the Base of the natural
   state.

4. FURTHER DOXOGRAPHICAL WORKS

Before moving to the description of the practice manual in section 5 below, one should note that several doxographical works included in the *Nyamgyü* (from the Dolpo version) discuss the structure of the *Six Lamps* and its ancillary texts. As we have seen in the introduction, the *Six Lamps* are included within the second main division of the *Zhangzhung Nyengyü*. This is however not always the case. Thus, according to Yangtön Pelzang, for instance, the *Six Lamps* should be included in the third part of the cycle, while other texts—generally ancillary works associated with the *Six Lamps*—are classified in the second division. I will give here the full translation of the two relevant sections in Yangtön Pelzang's *Expanded Text-List of the Oral Transmission of the Great Perfection in Zhangzhung (rDzogs pa chen po zhang zhung snyan rgyud kyi rtsis byang thems yig rgyas pa).* The text says (pp. 11–13):

> Second, the Inner Essential Instructions of the Precepts have five cycles of teachings. What are these?
> i. The Three Lamps of the summary,
> ii. The Four Lamps of the mode of arising (of visionary experiences),
> iii. The Six Essential Points of the real precepts,
> iv. The Three Short Treatises of oral advice, and
> v. The quintessential advice of the Heart of the Oral Transmission.
> These form the precept not to be disclosed to all other (beings) except for Single Transmission.

The Three Lamps of the summary are:

i. The Precepts on the Abiding Base,

ii. The Precepts on the experience of modes of arising, and

iii. The Precepts on the Fruit and the way to obtain it.[191]

As to the Four Lamps of the mode of arising, they are:

i. Sounds, rays, and lights that have no inherent nature,

ii. Sounds, rays, and lights as appearing in experiences and as signs of the Path,

iii. Sounds, rays, and lights as emerging due to sudden circumstances and

iv. Sounds, rays, and lights appearing during the time of bardo.

Such is the cycle of teachings regarding the Lamps of the mode of arising.[192]

Third, as to the Six Essential Points of the practice, they are:

i. The key point of identifying the Universal Base,

ii. The key point of the inner arising of our own Awareness,

iii. The key point of Transparent Wisdom,

iv. The key point of seeing Awareness in its nakedness,

v. The way of practicing the Path and the practice of deciding about the Three Bodies, and

vi. The practice during the time of the bardo.

(Fourth,) the Three Short Treatises are:

i. The direct introduction to sounds, rays, and lights while concentrating on the outer Lamp of existence,

191. This was translated with commentary in Achard, *The Three Precepts.*

192. This was translated with commentary in Achard, *The Four Lamps.*

ii. The pressure of the inner Water Lamp that is the eyes, and

iii. The Short Treatise on Meditation on the secret key points of channels and winds.

Such are the Three Short Treatises of Oral Advice.

Fifth, the two experiential precepts being the quintessential advice of the Heart of Oral Transmission are:

i. The cycle of the short examples of the Wheels and

ii. The Single Transmission of Oral Instructions.

The Wheels have four settings, which are:

i. The Wheel of the Abiding Base, set according to the short example of the complementary text,

ii. The Wheel of Interdependent Origination due to Realization or Delusion, set according to the short example of the complementary text,

iii. The Wheel of Channels Residing in the Body, set according to the short example of the complementary text, and

iv. The Wheel of the Time of the Bardo, set according to the short example of the complementary text.

Thus, this fourfold setting is called "The Setting of the Four Wheels."

The Single Transmission of Oral Instructions was not written down and is only to be known through the mouth of the master.

Since there is a commitment to this Oral Transmission,

It appeared as not being taught to all beings except for (those receiving) the Single Transmission.

Third, the cycle of teachings that disclose the secret Vision of
   Awareness in its nakedness

Deals with the Six Lamps, which are:

i. The Lamp of the Abiding Base, being the key point on how
   to identify the Universal Base and the expression of our
   Essence,

ii. The Lamp of the Flesh-Heart, being the key point to the
   inner arising of one's own Awareness and the basis on
   which it abides,

iii. The Lamp of the White and Smooth Channel, being the
   key point of the Transparent Wisdom and the path on
   which it arises,

iv. The Water Lamp of the Far-Reaching Lasso, being the key
   point of the vision of Awareness in its nakedness and the
   door to which it arises,

v. The Lamp of the Direct Introduction to the Pure Realms,
   being the key point of deciding upon the Three Bodies
   and how to practice the path, and

vi. The Lamp of the Moment of the Bardo, being the key point
   to the way saṃsāra and nirvāṇa separate and of reaching
   the boundaries between delusion and realization.

The six short treatises of advice associated with these Six
   Lamps,

Together with their related key points,

Are expounded as the secret cycle of teachings.

In another short work, Yangtön Pelzang describes the collection of works dealing with the combination of the *Six Lamps*
and the *Twenty-One Seals*. The translation of this work is as
follows:

From here, in the instructions concerning the Six Lamps and
the Twenty-One Seals,

There is the exposition of the origin of the lineage, meant to
develop faith,

And the meaning of the treatises that include quintessential
guidance and have three methods of practice.

In the practice of the meaning of the treatises
There are the six kinds of Lamps and
The twenty-one Seals:
The Lamp of the Abiding Base has eight kinds of Seals;
The Lamp of the Flesh-Heart,
The Lamp of the White and Smooth Channel, and
The Water Lamp of the Far Reaching Lasso,
Each has its Seal;
The Lamp of the Direct Introductions to the Pure Realms
has six Seals;
The Lamp of the Moment of the Bardo has two kinds of
Seals;
With these (equivalences) the obstacles of (potential) defects
(in the analysis of) the Lamps and Seals are removed.
With the twenty-first is exposed the principle of concretely
manifesting the Fruit of both the Lamps and the Seals.
In summary, if we condense (all the cycle), it consists of the
Lamps
And these can then be summed up to the Seals.

In the instructions on the Setting of the Four Wheels,
At the time of (exposing) the Lamp of the Abiding Base,
One should add the Wheel of the Abiding Base.
When explaining the Seals of the Eradication of Delusion,

One should add the Wheel of the interdependencies (creat-
ing) Realization and delusion.
When explaining the White and Smooth Channel
One should add the Wheel of the key points of the body and
channels,
And when (explaining) the Lamp of the Bardo,
One should add the Wheel of the Bardo.

Such are the oral instructions being written down.
These are at the present time the special instructions that
myself, Yangtön Pelzang, (have arranged).
Virtue! Ho! Ho![193]

5. THE PRACTICE MANUAL

In several editions, this practice manual is presented as having
three subdivisions: the Three Precepts (*Man ngag gsum*),[194] the
Four Lamps (*sGron ma bzhi*),[195] and the actual Six Essential
Points (*gNad drug*).[196] Since the first two divisions have already
been translated, commented upon, and studied in depth, we
shall concentrate here on the third part only.

The first of these Essential Points concerns the proper identification of the Base of the natural state. To proceed to this

---

193. This abstract is the afterword to Rangdröl Lama Gyeltsen's *Arrangement of the
Chapters of the Oral Transmission* (pp. 22–23).

194. Translated with commentary in Achard, *The Three Precepts*, Naldjor Institute,
2005.

195. Translated with commentary in Achard, *The Four Lamps*, Naldjor Institute,
2007.

196. Translated with commentary in Achard, *The Six Essential Points*, forthcoming.

correct identification, one should remain in the solitude of a hermitage and perform the preliminaries beforehand. Then, one should apply the four following key points:

- for the body, one sits in the fivefold position;
- for speech, one holds the breath, pressing down the upper wind and binding it to the lower wind;
- for the gaze, one gazes at the sky without moving the eyes; and
- for the mind, one remains free from the concerns of the past, present, and future.

After a few days of such a practice focused on sky gazing, one should directly experience the control of the mind and the dawn of Awareness. It is also possible that at that time, according to the practice manuals of the *Twenty-One Seals*,[197] some visions arise without effort.

In this condition, one experiences the Absolute Body (*bon sku*) by abiding in the direct nonduality of Clarity and Emptiness. At that time, several direct introductions (*ngo sprod*) should be given, such as the direct introduction to the Three Bodies (*sku gsum*), the sky (*nam mkha'*), Space (*dbyings*), the Expanse (*klong*), etc. Furthermore, following the nine methods explained in the *Twenty-One Seals*, one should progress rapidly in the various stages of the Path.[198]

197. I will come back to these texts in another book.

198. The complete explanation of the nine methods will be given in Achard, *The Twenty-One Seals*, forthcoming. Their list is the following: (1) the three Bindings, (2) the three Relaxations, (3) the three Methods of Resting, (4) the three Non-Followings, (5) the three Links, (6) the three Hidden Methods, (7) the three Arisings, (8) the three Liberations, and (9) the three Non-Obscurations.

The text then goes on with the description of the circumstances that lead to delusion, about which the author says:

> Thus when the manifested objects[199]
> Arise as sounds, lights, and rays,
> They are not recognized as the dynamism of Awareness.
> There is thus delusion when one sees the outer manifestations as having independent existence;
> For example, it is like when our form is reflected in water:
> When we don't understand that this is our own form
> (We take it) to arise as the form of something else.

Regarding the method for destroying delusion, the text says:

> When relying on the key points of the precepts, one contemplates the arising of the sounds, rays, and lights that are the secondary causes of delusion, but
> If one sees them as our illusory self-manifestations, the defects of delusion cannot be established.

In the second Essential Point, one is introduced to the practice of the inner arising of Self-Awareness. In fact, the text actually describes the sanctuary of the natural state within the body and identifies this location with the Brown Cornelian Tent (*mchong gur smug po*). It further says:

> Thus, even though the King of Awareness arises from within,

---

199. These are also known as the three manifestations (*snang ba gsum*), namely: sounds, lights, and rays.

It is for example like a treasure that one cannot see if there is
   no door (leading to it):
If one does not know how to contemplate the mind, Self-
   Awareness will not radiate;
Consequently, by relaxing the doorway of the Lamp in its
   natural condition,
One will directly contemplate the Essence of Awareness and
One will concretely realize the natural Clarity of Awareness
   as being ungraspable.

In the third Essential Point, the text describes a very powerful
method for being introduced to the Transparent Wisdom (*ye
shes zang thal*), which is certainly the "trademark" of this manual. One should sit in the fivefold posture and visualize the three
main channels within the body, press the stomach against the
spine, place the tongue against the palate, roll the eyes upward
and push the winds downward so as to have them enter the
central channel. At that time, one imagines that the essence of
one's mind and the winds are mixed into a single Thiglé, which is
blown upward as one exhales. This Thiglé shoots out of the upper
opening of the central channel and dissolves high into the sky.
At that time, one keeps one's Awareness focused on the sky. This
practice is the core of the yogic approach described in this text.

   In the fourth Essential Point, the author summarizes the process and reason for the arising of visions. He states that one's
natural state or Awareness, abiding in the heart, is endowed with
a luminous dynamism that arises inwardly through the pathway
of the channels and appears "outwardly" at the doorway of the
Lamps (the two eyes). If one remains naturally in a state free
from any activity, at that time Awareness will arise in its unborn
nature in an infinite variety of visionary manifestations. In

order to be directly introduced to this visionary Reality, which is the Clear-Light (*'od gsal*) itself, one presses the *Briguta* Lamps with the fingers while holding the breath. Then as one fills up the lungs with more air while maintaining the holding of the breath, many lights, rays, and various forms will be seen in their total nakedness. This is the direct introduction to one's own natural radiance (*rang mdangs*).

After that, while still holding the breath, one should push the air a little bit downward and release the pressure of the fingers. At that time, fivefold visionary lights will appear, as well as rainbows, etc. This second aspect corresponds to the introduction to one's own natural luminosity (*rang 'od*).

Eventually, one exhales the air totally and one keeps contemplating the visions without blocking or moving the doorways (the eyes) until these visions naturally disappear by themselves. This third aspect corresponds to the introduction to the natural dynamism (*rang rtsal*) of one's Awareness.

The fifth Essential Point is mainly concerned with various systems of direct introductions (*ngo sprod*) and with clear elucidation (*dmar thag gcod pa*) of the nature of the Three Bodies. At that point the text very abruptly mentions the natural existence (*rang chas*) of these Bodies within oneself but does not give any information. One has seen the main elements of this subject in the introduction to the present volume. This section is followed by that of the clear elucidation of these Three Bodies, which, at one point, contains a synthesis of the Thögel practice. The text says:

One concentrates Awareness on the sky, on the visions and
    the canopies of lights, or
One practices with the four essential points, namely:

The key point of the body (referring to the posture) held in a
state of nondistraction,

The key point of the senses (based on appropriate) Gazes,

The key point of the breath (consisting in the) entrance (of
winds inside the central channel), and

the key point of the mind (based on a) visualization; (practicing in this way),

Firstly, within the (visions of) Clear-Light will arise the
seeds of the Form Bodies and Thiglés

Similar to the multitude of stars shining in the sky.

After a while, when one has gained sufficient familiarization
with the practice, the visions of Clear-Light regularly intensify
as one progresses through the various stages during retreats.
We have seen above that these stages correspond to the Five
Visions, namely (1) the Increasing of Visions, (2) the Spreading
of Visions (3) the Intensification of Visions, (4) the Perfection
of Visions, and (5) the Ultimate Stage of Visions. All visionary
manifestations that are contemplated during these stages are
expressions of the dynamism of Awareness (*rig pa'i rtsal*) and are
devoid of inherent nature.

In the sixth and last Essential Point, the text describes the
mode of liberation (*grol tshul*) according to the three levels of
practitioners. Those of superior capacities reach Buddhahood
during their lifetime or at the time of their last breath. In the
latter case, it might be important to remind them of the instructions and to proceed with clarifications (*gsal 'debs*) about the
nature of the Mind. This sometimes comes as a necessity given
the circumstances eventually leading to death itself.

To those of intermediate capacities, teachings on the nature
of sounds, lights and rays are recited at the time of death and

after death. If their familiarization with the Thögel practice during their lifetime is sufficient, they are ascertained to recognize the nature of the visions appearing during the Bardo of Clear-Light (*'od gsal bar do*) and to reach Buddhahood thereafter.

Those of lower capacities are instructed in the practice of the Transfer (*Phowa*) and on the nature of the manifestations arising during the Bardo of Becoming (*srid pa'i bar do*). If their recognition is effective, then they are likely to perform the Transfer and take rebirth in a pure realm or a place where the teachings of the Buddha are maintained. After five hundred years of practice in this ultimate rebirth, they will reach final liberation.

Nothing is said of ordinary beings in the text but we have seen above that their ignorance will propel them into the Bardo of Becoming where they will helplessly face the retributions of their karma.

Glossary

Absolute Body (*bon gyi sku*)
The coalescence of Emptiness and Clarity abiding as the primordially pure mode of the natural state.

Awareness (*rig pa*)
The knowledge of the natural state (*gnas lugs*), independent from discursiveness, consciousnesses, intelligence, etc. It is not a "presence" but the actual direct knowledge of the Absolute Body (*bon sku*), which discerns itself exactly as it is. Rigpa is in fact the mode (*tshul*) of Mind itself (*sems nyid*), just like *marigpa* (ignorance) is the mode of the ordinary mind (*sems*).

Bardo (*bar do*)
An intermediate state between two other states, lasting for a determined duration. Generally, bardos are associated with the death and after-death processes, but this is a reductionist perspective since there are bardo states during the lifetime, such as the Bardo of the Sanctuary of Birth (*skye gnas kyi bar do*), the Bardo of Absorption (*ting 'dzin gyi bar do*), etc.

Base (*gzhi*)

The nature of the Mind expressed according to a primordially pure Essence, a spontaneously accomplished Nature, and an all-embracing Compassion.

Base of delusion (*'khrul gzhi*)

The mode of the Base when one does not recognize one's own nature, characterized by ignorance (*ma rig pa*).

Base of Liberation (*grol gzhi*)

The mode of the Base when one recognizes one's own nature, characterized by Awareness (*rig pa*).

Base of the natural state (*gzhi yi gnas lugs*)

The abiding mode of the real nature of the mind.

Black Guidance (*nag khrid*)

A type of instruction dealing with the practices to perform during dark retreats (*mun mtshams*). In the *Zhangzhung Nyengyü* the teachings belonging to this category are included in the *Seven Cycles of Clear-Light* (*'Od gsal bdun skor*).

Bodies (*sku*)

One of the two modalities (with Wisdoms) expressing the true essence of the natural state and the fruit of Buddhahood.

Body of the Great Transfer (*'pho ba chen po'i sku*)

One of the four forms of the Rainbow Body characterized by the fact that the yogi who reaches it does not show any signs of death and is not confronted with the postmortem bardo states. Very few masters have reached that level; among them in the Bönpo tradition are Tapihritsa, Drenpa Namkha, and Tsewang Rigdzin. It would seem that for many centuries nobody has manifested such a Body.

Brown Version (*sMug gu*)
One of the two subcycles of the extensive version of the *Nyamgyü*, together with the Grey Version.

Buddhahood (*sangs rgyas*)
The state of total enlightenment characterized by the natural display of Bodies and Wisdoms.

Chaktri (*Phyag khrid*)
The most important practice manual of the *Zhangzhung Nyengyü* compiled by Dru Gyelwa Yungdrung (1242–90) in seven chapters: (1) the history of the lineage, (2) the preliminaries, (3) the main practice, (4) instructions on the View, (5) instructions on Meditation, (6) instructions on Conduct, and (7) instructions on the Fruit.

Clarity (*gsal ba*)
One of the two modalities of the natural state, together with Emptiness.

Compassion (*thugs rje*)
The all-embracing (*kun khyab*) aspect of the natural state, defined as unceasing (*ma 'gag*).

Condensed version of the Experiential Transmission
(*Nyams rgyud bsdus pa*)
The shortest version of the *Nyamgyü*, including numerous complementary works, in particular all those associated with specific

"single transmission" (*gcig brgyud*) teachings. It is also known as the "miscellanea" (*thor bu*) because numerous short works have been added to the original set of texts in the course of time.

Cutting through Rigidity (*khregs chod*)
The practice consisting in cultivating the experience of the natural state, without artifice. It involves, after an initiatory stage, the capacity of integrating everything to this experience. Simply indulging in this experience without integration is of no use (for instance, at the time of death). See also below, under Trekchö.

Cycle of Dzogchen (*rdzogs chen skor*)
One of the two main subdivisions of the *Zhangzhung Nyengyü* collection, together with the Cycle of Secret Formulas (*gsang sngags skor*).

Cycle of Secret Formulas (*gsang sngags skor*)
One of the two main subdivisions of the *Zhangzhung Nyengyü* collection, together with the Cycle of Dzogchen (*rdzogs chen skor*).

Dark retreat (*mun mtshams*)
A dark retreat is one of the several techniques used during Thögel practice. In the *Zhangzhung Nyengyü*, the main practice of dark retreats follows the instructions collected in the *Seven Cycles of Clear-Light* (*'Od gsal bdun skor*). Generally, the retreat itself lasts for forty-nine days.

Dolpo
A region of northwestern Nepal, of Tibetan culture and language. This is the land of the Yangtön family lineage.

Drenpa Namkha (Dran pa nam mkha')

An eighth-century master who took part in the codification of New Bön teachings with Vairocana. According to the Bönpo tradition, there existed up to three Drenpa Namkhas: (1) Tazik Drenpa Namkha, a *siddha* whose main characteristics resemble those of Padmasambhava, (2) Zhangzhung Drenpa Namkha, one of the most important figures for the later Bön tradition, and (3) Böpa Drenpa Namkha, a Tibetan monk. There is considerable confusion as to the respective teachings that are attributed to these personages.

Dru Gyelwa Yungdrung (Bru rGyal ba g.yung drung, 1242–90)

Dru Gyelwa was one of the most important masters of the *Zhangzhung Nyengyü* lineage. He wrote an important practice manual in seven chapters associated with the cycle, entitled *Chaktri (Phyag khrid)*. He also wrote a commentary on the *Six Lamps*, which is the mostly used exegetical work during modern-day transmissions.

Dru lineage

A spiritual lineage associated with the Dru (Bru) family clan of Central Tibet.

Dynamism (*rtsal*)

The dynamism of the natural state is the expression of one's real nature arising as sounds (*sgra*), lights (*'od*), and rays (*zer*).

Dynamism of Awareness (*rig pa'i rtsal*)

This dynamism arises as sounds, lights, and rays at the time of the Base, when special circumstances are collected, during the practice of Thögel and during the Bardo of the Clear-Light of Reality.

Dzogchen (*rDzogs chen*)

The highest system of meditation in both the Bönpo and Nyingma school of Tibet. It stands as the ninth Vehicle within their Nine Ways scheme. It also designates the natural state of the individual.

Emanation Body (*sprul sku*)

The Body used by the Buddha Tönpa Shenrab and other Buddhas to manifest on this plane of existence. In the restricted context of Thögel meditation, this Body refers to all the visionary marvels that form the natural display of Awareness.

Emptiness (*stong pa*)

One of the two modalities of the natural state, together with Clarity.

Essence (*ngo bo*)

The Primordial Purity (*ka dag*) of the natural state, defined as empty (*stong pa*).

Eternal Bön (*g.yung drung bon*)

The "standard" or official tradition of Bön, said to originate with Buddha Tönpa Shenrab. The teachings of this tradition were diffused from Tazik Ölmo Lung-ring to Zhangzhung, Tibet, and other countries.

Exhaustion of the intellect and phenomena (*blo zad bon zad*)

Ultimate stage of the Path occurring during the fifth Vision of

Thögel practice according to the *Zhangzhung Nyengyü* teachings and resulting in the nonregressing realization of the Primordial Purity (*ka dag*) of one's genuine, natural state.

Experiential Transmission (*Nyams rgyud*)
The second subdivision of the Dzogchen section of the *Zhangzhung Nyengyü*. It is divided into the extended version (*rgyas
pa*), medium version (*'bring po*), and the condensed version
(*bsdus pa*), also known as "miscellanea" (*thor bu*). Contrary to
what some younger lamas assert, the *Chaktri* by Dru Gyelwa
does not belong to the Experiential Transmission but is a practice manual of the Oral Transmission (*snyan rgyud*).

Extensive version of the Experiential Transmission
(*Nyams rgyud rgyas pa*)
The long version of the *Nyamgyü* compiled by Yangtön Chenpo
and his sons, divided into two subcycles known as the Brown
Version (*sMug gu*) and the Grey Version (*sKya ru*).

Five Visions (*snang ba lnga*)
(1) The Increasing of Visions (*snang ba 'phel ba*), (2) the Spreading
of Visions (*snang ba mched pa*), (3) the Intensification of Visions
(*snang ba rgyas pa*), (4) the Perfection of Visions (*snang ba rdzogs
pa*), and (5) the Ultimate Stage of Visions (*snang ba mthar thug*).

Four Cycles of the Oral Transmission (*bKa' rgyud skor bzhi*)
Expression referring to the main Dzogchen section of the
Zhangzhung Nyengyü dealing with (1) the outer sections on the
View, (2) the inner section on essential precepts, (3) the secret
section on seeing Awareness in its nakedness, and (4) the inner-
most secret section on identifying the natural state.

Four key points (*gnad bzhi*)
(1) Doorways, (2) object, (3) breath, and (4) Awareness.

Four Lamps (*sgron ma bzhi*)
(1) The Lamp of the Far-Reaching Lasso (*rgyang zhags chu'i sgron ma*), (2) the Lamp of the Utterly Pure Space (*dbyings rnam par dag pa'i sgron ma*), (3) the Lamp of Empty Thiglés (*thig le stong pa'i sgron ma*), and (4) the Lamp of the Self-Arisen Sublime Knowledge (*shes rab rang byung gi sgron ma*).

Four Visions (*snang ba bzhi*)
(1) The Vision of Manifest Reality (*bon nyid mngon sum gyi snang ba*), (2) the Vision of Increased Luminous Experiences (*nyams snang gong 'phel gyi snang ba*), (3) the Vision of the Full Measure of Awareness (*rig pa tshad phebs kyi snang ba*), and (4) the Vision of the Exhaustion of Reality (*bon nyid zad pa'i snang ba*).

Fruit (*'bras bu*)
The result of the Path, expressed in the display of Bodies (*sku*) and Wisdoms (*ye shes*).

Gazes (*lta stangs*)
Manner of looking associated with the key point of doorways, namely directing the eyes upward, to the sides, or downward, depending on the posture that is being used.

Great Perfection (*rDzogs chen*)
See under Dzogchen.

Great Transfer (*'pho chen*)
See under Body of the Great Transfer.

Grey Version (*sKya ru*)
One of the two subcycles of the extensive version of the *Nyam-gyü*, together with the Brown Version.

Gyelzik Sechung (rGyal gzigs gSas chung)
The main disciple of Gyerpung Nangzher Löpo and his heir in the lineage of transmission.

Gyerpung Nangzher Löpo (Gyer spungs sNang bzher lod po)
An eighth-century figure central to the teachings of the *Zhang-zhung Nyengyü*. He is said to be the codifier of the cycle in the language of Zhangzhung and to have authored the commentary on the *Twenty-One Seals*. He is also one of the *Jalüpa* of this lineage of transmission, namely a master who achieved the Rainbow Body (*'ja' lus*) at the end of his life.

Ignorance (*ma rig pa*)
The deluded state of nonrecognition of one's natural state and of its manifestations.

Increasing of Visions (*snang ba 'phel ba*)
The first of the Five Visions.

Inner cycle (*nang skor*)
The second subdivision of the *Kagyü Korzhi* concerned with the essential precepts for practice. The root-text of this cycle is the *Six Lamps*, associated with its entire related works (commentaries, etc.).

Innermost secret cycle (*yang gsang skor*)
The fourth and last part of the *Kagyü Korzhi*, concerned with the direct identification of the natural state (*gnas lugs phug*

chod). Its main root-text is that of the *Twenty-One Seals* (*gZer bu nyer gcig*), which together with its ancillary texts constitute the core of Dzogchen teachings according to the *Zhangzhung Nyengyü*.

Instructions on the Six Lamps (*sGron ma drug gi gdams pa*)
The root-text of the inner section of the *Zhangzhung Nyengyü* describing the six following Lamps (*sgron ma*): (1) the Lamp of the Abiding Base, (2) the Lamp of the Flesh-Heart, (3) the Lamp of the White and Smooth Channel, (4) the Water Lamp of the Far-Reaching Lasso, (5) the Lamp of Direct Introductions to the Pure Realms, and (6) the Lamp of the Moment of the Bardo.

Intensification of Visions (*snang ba rgyas pa*)
The third of the Five Visions.

Intermediate version of the Experiential Transmission (*Nyams rgyud 'bring po*)
The medium-length version of the *Nyamgyü* divided into eight subcycles. This collection is very close to that of the extensive version.

Kagyü Korzhi (*bKa' rgyud skor bzhi*)
The Four Cycles of the Oral Transmission forming the main subdivisions of the cycle.

Kalpas (*bskal pa*)
Cosmic eras lasting billions of years.

Key point of mind (*sems kyi gnad*)
Concentrating on the eyes and fixing these on the sky.

Key point of speech (*ngag gi gnad*)
Silence combined with breathing through the mouth.

Key point of the body (*lus gnad*)
Generally, this refers to postures, either the five-points posture or the specific Thögel postures such as the position of the Lion, the Elephant, the Sage, the Swan, and the Antelope.

King of Awareness (*rig pa'i rgyal po*)
Awareness expressed as the ruler of all consciousnesses and in particular of the mental consciousness. Identical to the King of Self-Knowing Awareness (*rang shes rig gi rgyal po*). This Awareness is by no means a form of consciousness, since it precisely transcends consciousnesses, mental events, etc. It is the discerning Knowledge (*rig pa*) through which the natural state knows itself (*rang rig*).

King of Self-Knowing Awareness (*rang shes rig gi rgyal po*)
See under King of Awareness.

Knowledge Formulas (*rigs sngags*)
One of the three main subdivisions of the tantric instructions associated with the *Zhangzhung Nyengyü.*

Kuntuzangpo (*Kun tu bzang po*)
The primordial Enlightened One who is the source of the Dzogchen teachings. He is depicted as a blue naked Buddha, without ornaments.

Lopön Tenzin Namdak (Slob dpon bsTan 'dzin rnam dag, b. 1926)
He is one of the most influential masters of Dzogchen of his

generation. He was a head master in Menri before the Chinese invasion and founded the New Menri monastery in Dolanji (India) and that of Triten Norbutse (Nepal). His knowledge of Dzogchen is unequalled by anyone, and his dedication to the spread of Bön teachings is entirely unprecedented in the history of the lineage. He is now often referred to as Yongdzin Rinpoche.

Lower lineage (*smad lugs*)
Expression referring to the original lineage of the Experiential Transmission, as opposed to the Upper lineage (*smad lugs*) associated with the *Kagyü Korzhi*.

Makara (*chu srin*)
A mythological animal said to hold a gem in its mouth.

Manifestations of the Base (*gzhi snang*)
The spontaneous, dynamic arising of the manifestations of the natural state in their displays of sounds, lights, and rays.

Menri (sMan ri)
The name of the main Bönpo monastery, founded by Nyammé Sherab Gyeltsen in the fifteenth century. There are now two Menri monasteries: one in Tibet (the original one) and one in India constructed by the Bönpos in exile and directed by H.H. Lungtok Tenpai Nyima Rinpoche, the thirty-third abbot of Menri.

mind (*sems*)
The process of inner discursiveness.

Mind, Mind itself (*sems nyid*)
The nature of the mind.

Mind Series (*Sems sde*)
One of the three Series (*sde gsum*) of Dzogchen teachings, although the expression is not used in the Bön of Zhangzhung but rather in the tradition known as the "Bön of India" (*rgya gar gyi bon*).

Mu Tsoge (dMu Tsog ge)
A young disciple of Gyerpung and the main heir of Gyelzik Sechung.

Nangzher Löpo (sNang bzher lod po)
See under Gyerpung Nangzher Löpo.

Natural state (*gnas lugs*)
The original, primordial abiding mode of the Mind. This state is endowed with a primordially pure Essence, a spontaneously accomplished Nature, and an all-embracing Compassion.

Nature (*rang bzhin*)
The Spontaneous aspect (*lhun grub*) of the natural state, defined as luminous (*gsal ba*).

New Bön (*bon gsar*)
A Bönpo tradition said to go back to the eighth century when Drenpa Namkha and Vairocana codified its textual collections. These works started to be rediscovered later during the fourteenth century (with Tulku Loden Nyingpo, b. 1360) and throughout the following centuries, down to the present day.

Nirvāṇa (*'das pa*)
The unconditioned state beyond sorrow, characterized by realization, nongrasping.

Nyamgyü (*Nyams rgyud*)
See under Experiential Transmission.

Nyengyü (*sNyan rgyud*)
See under Oral Transmission of the Great Perfection in Zhangzhung.

Oral Transmission of the Great Perfection in Zhangzhung
(*rDzogs pa chen po zhang zhung snyan rgyud*)
The main Dzogchen cycle of the Bönpo tradition. It is divided into four main sections: (1) the View, (2) the Precepts, (3) the naked vision of Awareness, and (4) the identification of the natural state.

Oral Transmission of Zhangzhung (*Zhang zhung snyan rgyud*)
See the preceding entry and under *Zhangzhung Nyengyü*.

Outer cycle (*phyi skor*)
The first cycle of the *Kagyü Korzhi* dealing with the general sections on the View (*lta ba spyi gcod*). The root-text of this cycle is the *Twelve Little Son-Tantras* (*rgyud bu chung bcu gnyis*). Several ancillary texts comment upon the contents of this root-text, together with a few protohistorical works. All of these form the "outer cycle."

Passing over the Crest (*thod rgal*)
The Dzogchen practice of Clear-Light (*'od gsal*), centered

around six key points involving special postures, gazes, breathing techniques, etc. During this practice, one is confronted with Four Visions (*snang ba bzhi*) that are signs indicating the intensity of one's integration of Awareness (*rig pa*), these visions being variously intensified manifestations of the glow of Awareness (*rig pa'i gdangs*). This practice leads ultimately to the sixteenth stage of the Path and to the Fruit of the Rainbow Body (*'ja' lus*). See also below, under Thögel.

Path (*lam*)

The gradual stages that one goes through during the practice. In the context of the *Zhangzhung Nyengyü*, the Path is mostly concerned with the practice of the preliminaries, the inner Rushen, Trekchö (*khregs chod*), and Thögel (*thod rgal*).

Patön Tengyel Zangpo
(sPa bsTan rgyal bzang po, fourteenth century)
A very important lineage holder of the Pa family clan. He has authored numerous influential works, such as his history of the *Zhangzhung Nyengyü*, a more general history of Bön, etc. His dates are uncertain but some think he lived during the fourteenth century and others, a little bit later.

Perfection Body (*rdzogs sku*)
The spontaneous aspect (*lhun grub*) of one's nature (*rang bzhin*), abiding in fivefold displays and multicolored manifestations. It is the first of the two Form Bodies (*gzugs sku gnyis*).

Perfection of Visions (*snang ba rdzogs pa*)
The fourth of the Five Visions.

Pönchen Tsenpo (dPon chen bTsan po)
He is apparently an historical figure who must have lived in the
late tenth–early eleventh centuries. He is presented as the master who translated the *Zhangzhung Nyengyü* from the language
of Zhangzhung into Tibetan. He is also the author of the root
Yantras of the cycle.

Precepts in Eight Chapters (*Man ngag le'u brgyad pa*)
The root-text of the third section of the *Zhangzhung Nyengyü*
dealing with the naked vision of Awareness (*rig pa gcer mthong*).
It is arranged according to the following themes: (1) the Precept on the Abiding Base, (2) the manifest existence of Buddhahood in our continuum, (3) the Essence of the Absolute
Body as existing in oneself, (4) the characteristics of the Absolute Body, (5) the direct introductions to the Pure Realms of
the Buddhas, (6) the Contemplation of the principles of the
natural state, (7) the principles of Non-Meditation, and (8)
the mode of liberation of excellent, medium, and ordinary
yogis.

Precepts in Twelve Chapters (*Man ngag le'u bcu gnyis pa*)
One of the texts belonging to the first section of the *Zhangzhung Nyengyü* and concerned with the following themes: (1)
the generic Base of saṃsāra and nirvāṇa, (2) the Base of Liberation of Buddhas, (3) the mode of delusion, (4) the transcendence of the ultimate Fruit, (5) the general classifications of
the Path, (6) the direct introduction to the Wisdom of Awareness, (7) the manner of introducing people to an instantaneous
understanding, (8) the manner in which the ultimate Fruit liberates, (9) the manner in which realized Buddhas liberate, (10)
the mode of delusion as a result of not realizing the Base, (11)

the Classifications of the Path, and (12) the excellences of the Great Perfection.

Precepts Series (*Man ngag sde*)
One of the three Series (*sde gsum*) of Dzogchen teachings, although not used in the Bön of Zhangzhung but rather in the tradition known as the "Bön of India" (*rgya gar gyi bon*). The main practices performed in this Precepts Section are the cultivation of the natural state (styled Trekchö in the Indian tradition) and the practice of Clear-Light (styled Thögel in the Indian tradition).

Primordial Purity (*ka dag*)
The Primordial Purity refers to the Essence of the natural state, which is defined as empty and stainless from the beginning.

Rainbow Body (*'ja' lus*)
The Rainbow Body is a sign occurring at the end of the Path of Dzogchen. It indicates that the level of the Perfection Body (*rdzogs sku*) has been attained and that the Mind is about to dissolve into its true Essence, which is the Absolute Body (*bon sku*). In general, it is said that there exists up to four kinds of Rainbow Bodies: (1) the Great Transfer (*'pho ba chen po*), (2) the Great Rainbow Body (*'ja' lus chen po*), (3) the Small Transfer (*'pho ba chung ngu*), and (4) the Small Rainbow Body (*'ja' lus chung ngu*). These are however not discussed in the *Zhangzhung Nyengyü* nor, to my knowledge, in Bönpo literature.

Refined Gold of the Great Perfection (*rDzogs chen gser zhun*)
An important cycle of Dzogchen teachings revealed by Yungdrung Pema Tsewang Gyelpo.

Sādhana (*grub thabs*)
A "method of accomplishment" or text describing the various stages of a given tantric practice.

Saṃsāra (*'khor ba*)
The state of conditioned existence.

Sang-ngak Lingpa (gSang sngags gling pa, 1864–1959?)
He was one of the most influent Tertön (*gter ston*) of his time and both a master and a disciple of Shardza Rinpoche to whom he handed over numerous Treasure transmissions. He was also a disciple of several recent and important masters such Patön Tenpa Drugdrak and Ratön Kelzang Tenpai Gyeltsen. His gigantic contributions to Bön teachings include his famed *Heart Drops of Jamma* (*Byams ma snying thig*) and numerous other works such as the *Tantra of the Three Bodies* (*sKu gsum don rgyud*).

Secret Cycle (*gsang skor*)
The third subdivision of the *Kagyü Korzhi*, dealing with the Vision of Awareness in its nakedness (*rig pa gcer mthong*) and concerned with the one and only text of this section: the *Precepts in Eight Chapters* (*Man ngag le'u brgyad pa*).

Secret Formulas (*gsang sngags*)
One of the three main subdivisions of the tantric instructions associated with the *Zhangzhung Nyengyü*.

Self-Arisen Wisdom (*rang byung ye shes*)
The Primeval Knowledge being equivalent with Awareness (*rig pa*).

Shardza Rinpoche (Shar rdza bKra shis rgyal mtshan, 1859–1934)
One of the most important masters of the Bön tradition. He authored numerous works and reached the Rainbow Body in 1934.

Single Thiglé (*thig le nyag gcig*)
The unitary expression of the natural state. Its aspect of singularity or unicity means that it transcends all dualities, such as the two truths, etc. Its abiding as a Thiglé is simply an expression of its perfection illustrated by its absence of edges, etc.

Single transmission (*gcig brgyud*)
Tradition consisting in the transmission of the Dzogchen teachings of the *Zhangzhung Nyengyü* to a single disciple only. Formal transmissions may be handed over to several students but the main official transmission is given only to the heir in the lineage. There are several lines of this single transmission still existing today.

Space (*dbyings*)
The intangible spiritual domain in which the visions of the natural state arise and manifest.

Space of the Universal Base (*kun gzhi'i dbyings*)
The Space of the Single Thiglé embracing all beings without exception. This state is illustrated by the sky without limit, which embraces everything.

Space Series (*Klong sde*)
One of the three Series (*sde gsum*) of Dzogchen teachings, although not used in the Bön of Zhangzhung but rather in the tradition known as the "Bön of India" (*rgya gar gyi bon*).

Spontaneity (*lhun grub*)

The notion of Spontaneity refers to the Nature (*rang bzhin*) of the primordial state and to its luminous aspect. It thus concerns the arising mode of the state and its dynamism. It has nothing to do with Conduct as some deluded people think. Spontaneity precisely refers to the luminous nature of our mind and to its potential expressed in the variety of its arising modes (lights, Thiglés, etc.)

Spreading of Visions (*snang ba mched pa*)

The second of the Five Visions.

Supports (*rten*)

In the context of Thögel practice, these supports are the sky, the rays of the sun, the moon, butter lamps, and the darkness of a dark cell (*mun khang*).

Tapihritsa (eighth century)

The twenty-fifth lineage holder of the *Zhangzhung Nyengyü* tradition. He was a disciple of Tsepung Dawa Gyeltsen and the main master of Gyerpung Nangzher Löpo. He is probably the most important figure of the cycle and is said to have reached the Body of the Great Transfer (*'pho ba chen po'i sku*), the highest level of realization for a Dzogchen practitioner.

Terma (*gTer ma*)

Texts, objects, or substances hidden by an enlightened master, to be revealed in future times by predestined individuals called Treasure Revealers (*gter ston*).

This-ngak (*this sngags*)
One of the three main subdivisions of the tantric instructions associated with the *Zhangzhung Nyengyü*.

Thögel (*thod rgal*)
One of the two central practices of Dzogchen, together with Trekchö. The practice of Thögel is based on the contemplation of the dynamism of Awareness (*rig pa'i rtsal*) in ever-increasing visions (*snang ba*). The classical, literal meaning of Thögel is that of passing (*rgal*) over the crest (*thod*). In the *Zhangzhung Nyengyü* collected instructions, Thögel is described at length in chapters 3 (part II) and 5 of the *Chaktri* (*Phyag khrid*).

Three Bodies (*sku gsum*)
The Absolute Body (*bon sku*), the Perfection Body (*rdzogs sku*), and the Emanation Body (*sprul sku*).

Three manifested objects (*snang yul gsum*)
Sounds (*sgra*), lights (*'od*), and rays (*zer*), the three manifestations pertaining to the dynamism of Awareness.

Three Realms (*khams gsum*)
The Desire Realm, the Form Realm, and the Formless Realm.

Tönpa Shenrab (sTon pa gshen rab)
The founder of the Eternal Bön tradition (*g.yung drung bon*).

Treasury of Space and Awareness (*dByings rig mdzod*)
The *magnum opus* of Shardza Rinpoche in twenty-one chapters, dealing with all aspects of Dzogchen knowledge and practice

according to the Bönpo tradition. This is one of the most important works of all Dzogchen teachings.

Trekchö (*khregs chod*)

One of the two central practices of Dzogchen, together with Thögel. The practice of Trekchö implies the uncontrived cultivation of the natural state and its stabilization without artifices. The classical, literal meaning of Trekchö is that of cutting (*chod*) through rigidity (*khregs*). In the *Zhangzhung Nyengyü* collected instructions, Trekchö is described at length in chapters 3 (part I) and 4 of the *Chaktri* (*Phyag khrid*).

Trisong Detsen (Khri srong lde btsan)

King of Tibet, described by the Buddhists as a *dharmarāja* and by the Bönpos as a persecutor of their faith. His role in the *Zhangzhung Nyengyü* is mentioned in a text entitled the *Reasons Why Bön Was Not Abolished* (*Bon ma nub pa'i gtan tshigs*) which most evidently compiles ancient material similar to that found in the Dunhuang caves but placed under the reign of another king.

Tsepung Dawa Gyeltsen (Tshe spungs Zla ba rgyal mtshan)

The twenty-fourth lineage holder of the *Zhangzhung Nyengyü* and the master of both Tapihritsa and Gyerpung Nangzher Löpo. He is said to have reached the Rainbow Body at the end of his life.

Tsewang Rigdzin (Tshe dbang rig 'dzin, eighth century)

A very important figure in the later, postdynastic Bönpo tradition. He is the eldest son of Drenpa Namkha and appears as an Immortal manifesting himself to worthy vessels to whom he entrusts teachings. His role in the later *Terma* tradition is crucial, much like that of his father.

Twelve Son-Tantras (*rgyud bu chung bcu gnyis*)
The root-text of the first section of the *Zhangzhung Nyengyü* dealing with the main principles of the View (*lta ba*).

Twenty-One Seals (*gZer bu nyer gcig*)
The root-text of the fourth section of the *Zhangzhung Nyengyü* dealing with the direct identification of the natural state. It has one commentary whose authorship is attributed to Gyerpung Nangzher Löpo.

Ultimate Stage of Visions (*snang ba mthar thug*)
The fifth of the Five Visions.

Universal Base (*kun gzhi*)
The Base (*gzhi*) of all (*kun*) manifestations of saṃsāra and nirvāṇa. Not to be confounded with the consciousness of the Universal Base (*kun gzhi rnam shes*), which corresponds to *ālayavijñāna*, the consciousness-store of all karmic impregnations.

Upper lineage (*stod lugs*)
Expression referring to the original lineage of the *Kagyü Korzhi*, as opposed to the Lower lineage (*smad lugs*) associated with the Experiential Transmission. "Upper" and "Lower" are geographical adjectives.

View (*lta ba*)
The theoretical explanation of the natural state's abiding mode. This View explains the fundamentals of Clarity and

Emptiness, the principles of the Universal Base (*kun gzhi*), Awareness (*rig pa*), and mind (*sems*). The teachings on the View in the *Zhangzhung Nyengyü* are contained in the outer cycle (*phyi skor*) as well as in the *Chaktri*, in chapters 3 (part I) and 4.

Vision of Awareness in its nakedness (*rig pa gcer mthong*)
Expression referring to the third section of the *Kagyü Korzhi* and dealing with the *Precepts in Eight Chapters*.

Wisdom of Self-Awareness (*rang rig ye shes*)
The Wisdom of the natural state abiding in the heart of all sentient beings. It is the totally pure Knowledge of the real nature of Mind.

Wisdoms (*ye shes*)
One of the two modalities (with Bodies) expressing the true essence of the natural state and the fruit of Buddhahood.

Yangtön lineage
A spiritual lineage associated with the Yangtön (Yang ston) family clan of Dolpo. As shown by D. Snellgrove, Yangtön is the abbreviation of Ya-ngal gyi ston pa, "teachers of the Ya-ngal" clan.

Yangtön Sherab Gyeltsen (Yang ston Shes rab rgyal mtshan)
An eleventh-century figure who played a key role in the transmission of the Dzogchen teachings. He is also deeply associated with the Experiential Transmission, which he partly wrote down, based on the teachings of his master Orgom Kündül.

Yongdzin Rinpoche (Yongs 'dzin rin po che)
A title of Lopön Tenzin Namdak.

Yongdzin Sangye Tendzin (Yongs 'dzin Sangs rgyas bstan 'dzin, 1912–78)
One of the two root-masters of Lopön Tenzin Namdak Rinpoche. He was a highly learned and highly realized lineage holder of the *Zhangzhung Nyengyü*, which he received from the Menri abbot Tenpa Lodrö Rinpoche. He was also a lineage holder of the Magyü or Mother Tantras (*Ma rgyud*).

Zhangzhung (Zhang zhung)
Ancient kingdom situated in what is now Western Tibet, with a capital known as Khyunglung Ngülkhar, the Silver Castle of the Garuda Valley. This kingdom was conquered during the reign of Songtsen Gampo according to Dunhuang documents, and during the reign of Trisong Detsen according to the later Bönpo tradition. To reconcile both theories, there is now a new version of the history stating that there were two conquests of Zhangzhung, but this is very unlikely.

Zhangzhung Meri (Zhang zhung Me ri)
The main Yidam of the *Zhangzhung Nyengyü.*

Zhangzhung Nyengyü (Zhang zhung snyan rgyud)
A collection of texts comprising tantric and Dzogchen teachings. It is also the generic expression used to refer to the *Kagyü Korzhi* in order to distinguish it from the *Nyamgyü* sets of works.

Bibliography

Achard, Jean-Luc

Les Quatre Cycles de la Transmission Orale de la Grande Perfection au Zhang-zhung (bKa' rgyud skor bzhi), Khyung-mkhar, 1991.

Les Instructions sur les Six Lampes, Zhangzhung Nyengyü, Horssérie no. 2, Khyung-mkhar, 1996.

The Three Precepts, Zhangzhung Nyengyü Studies, vol. 1, Naldjor Institute for Movement, München, 2005.

Les Prophéties de Tapihritsa, Editions Khyung-Lung, Sumène, 2005.

La Structure du Zhangzhung Nyengyü, Editions Khyung-Lung, Sumène, 2006.

The Dawn of Awareness: The Practice Manual for the Special Preliminaries of Dzogchen, Zhangzhung Nyengyü Studies, vol. 2, Naldjor Institute for Movement, München, 2006.

The Four Lamps, Zhangzhung Nyengyü Studies, vol. 3, Naldjor Institute for Movement, München, 2007.

La Pratique des Six Points Essentiels de l'Esprit de Parfaite Pureté, volume I, Editions Khyung-Lung, Sumène, 2007.

La Lampe Clarifiant les Conseils sur la Base Universelle, Editions Khyung-Lung, Sumène, 2009.

"Mesmerizing with the Useless? A book-review inquiry into the ability to properly reprint older worthy material," in *Revue d'Etudes Tibétaines*, no. 19, October 2010, pp. 133–43.

The Precepts in Eight Chapters, Zhangzhung Nyengyü Studies, vol. 4, Naldjor Institute for Movement, Münich, 2011.

La Biographie de Lopön Tenzin Namdak Rinpoche, volume I, Editions Khyung-Lung, Sumène, 2011.

The Instructions on the Primordial A—The Fifteen Sessions of Practice, Guru-Yoga, Instructions without Characteristics and Phowa Teachings, Vajra Publications, Kathmandu, 2012, 87 pages.

The Basic Structure of the Zhangzhung Nyengyü According to the Menri Edition, Khyung-mkhar, 2012, pdf ed., 14 pages.

Les Corps d'Arc-en-ciel et leur interprétation selon Düdjom Rinpoche, Khyung-mkhar, 2012, pdf ed., 8 pages.

Bönpo Newsletter, no. 21 (January 2012), p. 3.

Anonymous

rDzogs pa chen po zhang zhung snyan rgyud kyi bka' rgyud skor bzhi'i 'chad thabs, Kanjur (A yong bka' 'gyur ed.), vol. 110, pp. 27–54.

Baroetto, Giuseppe

Il Libro Tibetano dei Sei Lumi, Ubaldini Editore, Roma, 2002.

Blezer, Henk

"Greatly Perfected in Space and Time: Historicities of the Bon Aural Transmission from Zhang zhung," in R. Vitali (ed.), *The Earth Ox Papers, Proceedings of the International*

Seminar on Tibetan and Himalayan Studies, Tibet Journal,
Autumn 2009, vol. XXXIV n. 3 – Summer 2010, vol. XXXV,
n. 3, pp. 71–160.

"'Light' on the Human Body—The Coarse Physical Body and
Its Functions in the *Aural Transmission from Zhang zhung on
the Six Lamps,*" *Revue d'Etudes Tibétaines*, no. 23, April 2012,
pp. 117–68.

Bönpo Tengyur

Bon gyi brten 'gyur chen mo, compiled by dKar ru grub dbang
sprul sku bsTan pa'i nyi ma, Lha sa, 1998, 333 volumes.

Dru Gyelwa Yungdrung (1242–90)

*The Commentary on the Contemplative Meaning of the Six Lamps
Extracted from the Oral Transmssion of the Great Perfection in
Zhangzhung (rDzogs pa chen po zhang zhung snyan rgyud las
sgron ma drug gi dgongs don 'grel pa)*, Gangs ti se bon gzhung,
rTse zhig dgon vol. 24, pp. 217–63.

'Bras bu rang sar bzung ba sku gsum dmar thag bcad pa'i khrid,
Gangs ti se bon zhung, rTse-zhig dgon, vol. 20, pp. 363–70.

Duff, Tony

*About the Three Lines that Strike Key Points by Dodrupchen III
Tenpa'i Nyima, An Explanation of the Thorough Cut with
Direct Crossing Woven in*, Padma Karpo Translation Com-
mittee, 2009.

Germano, David

*The Experiential Transmission of Drugyelwa Yungdrung, Part
One: The Nine Phases of the Preliminary Spiritual Practices*

within the Zhang Zhung Oral Lineage of the Great Perfection, Ligmincha Institute, 1994.

Keutzer, Kurt

Chapter Four—The Base: Self-Introduction and Guidance on the View of Naked Seeing, Ligmincha Institute, 2003.

Chapter Five—The Practice of the Path: Guidance on the Stages of Meditation on Clear Light, Ligmincha Institute, 2005.

Guidance on Behavior—Working With the Dynamic Energy Through Integrating Causal Conditions Into the Path, Ligmincha Institute, s.d. (2006).

The Fruition—The Guidance That Delivers the Profound Certainty That the Three Enlightened Bodies Are Within You, Ligmincha Institute, 2007.

Texts of the Zhang zhung snyan rgyud Cycle of Teachings, n.p., unpublished, 2010.

Kvaerne, Per

The Stages of A-khrid Meditation, Dzogchen Practice of the Bon Tradition, by Bru-sgom rGyal-ba g.yung-drung (1242–90), translated by Per Kvaerne and Thupten K. Rikey, Library of Tibetan Works and Archives, Dharamsala, 1996.

Martin, Dan (et al.)

A Catalogue of the Bon Kanjur, National Museum of Ethnology, 2003, Bon Studies 8, Senri Ethnological Reports 40, Osaka, 2003.

Orofino, Giacomella

Sacred Tibetan Teachings on Death and Liberation, Prism Press, Bridport, 1990.

Rangdröl Lama Gyeltsen

Arrangement of the Chapters of the Oral Transmission: sNyan rgyud le'u'i sgrigs kha, Zhang zhung snyan rgyud kyi rnam thar chen mo sogs dang brgyud phyag bcas kyi gsung pod, A Collection of texts of the Bonpo *Zhang Zhung Snyan rgyud* precepts of rdzogs-chen practice, reproduced from a manuscript from the Samling Monastery in Dolpo (northwestern Nepal) by Yongs-dzin Sangs-rgyas bstan-'dzin Tibetan Bonpo Monastic Centre, Dolanji, 1974, pp. 17–23.

Reynolds, John Myrdhin

The Practice of Dzogchen in the Zhang-zhung Tradition of Tibet, Translations from the (sic!) The Gyalwa Chaktri of Druchen Gyalwa Yungdrung, and the Seven Fold Cycle of the Clear Light, Vajra Publications, Kathmandu, 2011.

Rossi, Donatella

The Philosophical View of the Great Perfection of the Bonpos, Snow Lion, 1999.

Shardza Rinpoche (bKra shis rgyal mtshan, 1859–1934)

sKu gsum rang shar: rDzogs pa chen po sku gsum rang shar, Gangs ti se bon gzhung, vol. 21, rTse-zhig dgon, 2008.

dByings rig rin po che'i mdzod, vol. 1–2, bDe chen ri khrod par ma (xylographic ed.), s.d.

'Bras bu rang sar bzung ba'i khrid 'khor 'das mnyam sbyor, sKu gsum rang shar, pp. 153–70.

Snellgrove, David

The Nine Ways of Bon, London Oriental Series vol. 18, London, 1967.

Uri Sönam Gyeltsen (thirteenth century)

Ornament of Solar Lights: A Commentary on the Lamps Extracted from the Oral Transmission of the Great Perfection in Zhangzhung (rDzogs pa chen po zhang zhung snyan rgyud las sgron ma'i 'grel nyi 'od rgyan), Gangs ti se bon gzhung, vol. 24, pp. 264–305.

Wangyal, Tenzin

Wonders of the Natural Mind, Station Hill Press, 1993; reprinted under the same title by Snow Lion, 2000.

Yangtön Pelzang (thirteenth century)

The Extended List containing the Enumeration of works belonging to the Oral Transmission of the Great Perfection in Zhangzhung: rDzogs pa chen po zhang zhung snyan rgyud kyi rtsis byang thems yig rgyas pa, in Zhang zhung snyan rgyud kyi rnam thar chen mo sogs dang brgyud phyag bcas kyi gsung pod, A Collection of texts of the Bonpo *Zhang Zhung Snyan rgyud* precepts of rdzogs-chen practice, reproduced from a manuscript from the Samling Monastery in Dolpo (northwestern Nepal) by Yongs-dzin Sangs-rgyas bstan-'dzin Tibetan Bonpo Monastic Centre, Dolanji, 1974, pp. 1–16.

Yongdzin Lopön Tenzin Namdak Rinpoche

History and Doctrine of Bon po Nispanna Yoga, Satapitaka Series, vol. 73, New Delhi, 1968.

The Main Dzogchen Practices, ed. by Gerd Manusch, Zhangzhung Nyen Gyü Manual, vol. 3, Naldjor Institute, 2005.

The Meditation on the Clear-Light, ed. by Gerd Manusch, Zhangzhung Nyen Gyü Manual, vol. 4, Naldjor Institute, 2005.

Zhangzhung Nyengyü

Man ngag le'u bcu gnyis pa, Gangs ti se bon gzhung, vol. 24, pp. 114–28.

sGron ma drug gi gdams pa, pp. 202–16; *History and Doctrines of Bon po Nispanna Yoga*, pp. 269–92; dBal khyung dgon *bKa' 'gyur*, vol. 171, pp. 181–230; bSam gling mss, 24 folios (pp. 563–98 of the Menri photocopy); A yong *bKa' 'gyur*, vol. 110, pp. 171–92; Nyarong ed., photographs 111–27.

Index

About the Author

Jean-Luc Achard is a Tibetologist, researcher at the Centre National de la Recherche Scientifique (CNRS, France), and the editor and publisher of the *Revue d'Etudes Tibétaines*, a free online academic journal of Tibetan Studies. He has been studying Buddhism for thirty-five years and has specialized in the study and practice of the teachings of Dzogchen (Great Perfection). In particular, he has studied with Yongdzin Lopön Tenzin Namdak Rinpoche for several years and translated numerous Bönpo texts on Dzogchen for retreats led by Yong-dzin Rinpoche. He is currently engaged in the translations and commentaries of several key works on Dzogchen belonging to the Bön and Nyingma traditions of Tibetan Buddhism.

Also Available from Wisdom Publications

Heart of the Great Perfection
Dudjom Lingpa's Visions of the Great Perfection
B. Alan Wallace

Includes *The Sharp Vajra of Conscious Awareness Tantra, Essence of Clear Meaning, The Foolish Dharma of an Idiot Clothed in Mud and Feathers*, and *The Enlightened View of Samantabhadra*.

Stilling the Mind
Shamatha Teachings from Dudjom Linpa's Vajra Essence
B. Alan Wallace

"A much needed, very welcome book."—Jetsün Khandro Rinpoche

The Flight of the Garuda
Dzogchen Teachings of Tibetan Buddhism
Keith Dowman

"I heartily recommend it."—Lama Surya Das, author of *Awakening the Buddha Within*

Natural Perfection
Longchenpa's Radical Dzogchen
Keith Dowman

"Dowman offers the essence of Dzogchen stripped of any cultural trappings. Like Alan Watts's Zen, it's distinguished by its transcendence of the other aspects of Buddhist practice."
—*Buddhadharma*

Original Perfection
Vairotsana's Five Early Transmissions
Keith Dowman
Foreword by Bhakha Tulku Pema Rigdzin

A beautiful, lyrical translation of the first five Dzogchen texts with crystal-clear commentary.

Buddhahood in This Life
The Great Commentary by Vimalamitra
Malcolm Smith

A complete translation of the earliest Tibetan commentary on the Dzogchen secret instructions.

Journey to Certainty
The Quintessence of the Dzogchen View: An Exploration of Mipham's Beacon of Certainty

"Remarkably accessible, this book is essential reading for anyone attempting to understand or practice Dzogchen today."
—John Makransky, author of *Awakening Through Love*

About Wisdom Publications

Wisdom Publications is the leading publisher of classic and contemporary Buddhist books and practical works on mindfulness. To learn more about us or to explore our other books, please visit our website at wisdomexperience.org or contact us at the address below.

Wisdom Publications
199 Elm Street
Somerville, MA 02144 USA

We are a 501(c)(3) organization, and donations in support of our mission are tax deductible.

Wisdom Publications is affiliated with the Foundation for the Preservation of the Mahayana Tradition (FPMT).